GW00383218

GREENSHIELDS
A Glasgow Cop
End of an Era

My name is William Greenshields,
a.k.a. *'That Bastard Greenshields'*

William Greenshields

Contents

This book is dedicated
to my sister Elizabeth 'Betty' Mills.

The author at work

Contents

Bain Street

A drugs dealer at the Barras

I'm a spiteful and resentful little sod at the best of times, when I take a dislike to some-one, particularly a criminal, I'll go out of my way to do he or she a very, very bad turn.

So it was with great delight that I received a bit of information from an acquaintance of mine who owned a shop at the Barras.

An old adversary *'Robin'*, mentioned on page 62 of *'Greenshields - a Glasgow Cop'* was selling *'smack'*, heroin, from a flat at number 8 Bain Street which was at that time occupied by his mother, brother, sister and himself.

The father was deceased and no great loss to society.

The flat is located on the first floor of a tenement block which stands at the corner of Bain Street and Gallowgate on the outskirts of the Barras market and overlooked the Victorian public toilets in Bain Square before they were concreted over.

My informant was quite explicit in describing how Robin was conducting his business.

The *'shop'* would open soon after 10a.m. every day, with a constant stream of callers who would have to buzz up to the flat by using the controlled entry intercom system which was located on the left side of the wall at the front door at street level.

Only when the occupant was satisfied with the identity of the caller would the door to the close be opened and the customer admitted.

Trade would continue for most of the day, ending about 6p.m.

I would have to take a look for myself but do it very carefully as I am well known in the area although I still don't receive any Birthday or Christmas cards from the inhabitants. Must have been something I said!

Dressing down for the occasion from my obligatory lounge suit would be advisable. All C.I.D. officers were required to dress smartly in a suit, collar and tie when on day-shift and were allowed to be slightly more casually dressed in a jacket, trousers, collar and tie when on late or night shift.

I wouldn't have considered attempting surveillance whilst wearing a suit anyway. If you wore a suit in the Calton you were either a cop, a debt collector or a Mormon missionary. I'll never be a missionary, if I do actually possess a soul it may just be a tad on the tainted side. Hell will be an interesting place, many *'friends'* will already be there and are no doubt anxious to greet me. Even the devil himself could learn a few dirty tricks from me when I finally meet my mentor.

I telephoned an acquaintance who had access to an unoccupied flat at the Barras which overlooked the entrance to the close in question, if I could get myself into the flat without being recognised I would be in a position to observe the dealing and maybe even put names to some of the faces who were buying the drugs from Robin.

I spoke with the grumpy old Det/Inspector, telling him of my information and got the go-ahead with the proviso that if I watched the close at number 8 Bain Street for two days at most and nothing untoward was seen to be occurring there then we would simply pull the plug on the operation.

I would then revert to my *'Ralph Slater'* suit and go back to the mundane run of the mill enquiries.

A couple of days later, armed with a set of house keys for what I discovered to be a rather smelly top floor tenement flat I took my place behind the dirty net curtains and waited there equipped with a set of binoculars, notepad, pencil and a police issue radio which I'd turned off. No point in creeping unseen into the flat and then giving the game away by the radio announcing to the other occupants of the block that a police officer was in the building.

It would only be turned on if for some reason assistance was required in a hurry.

The door to number 8 Bain Street which was directly across the road from my observation point consisted of a wooden frame with four glass panels inset and afforded me of a fairly good view of the interior of the close when looked at through my binoculars.

It was about 8.30a.m. on a Wednesday morning and my week-end off was looming, Thursday was my last working day before the night shift began the following Monday.

I wanted to do this deed before the week-end interrupted me and it would have to be placed on the back-burner until after I returned to day-shift ten days later.

Unusually, it went like clockwork, the callers; all with the gaunt 'junkie' appearance began arriving soon after 10a.m. and were using the door entry system just as my informant had reported.

Neither Robin nor any of his family had made an appearance as yet. None of the family had left the building and I'd been in position for the best part of two hours. The rear door from the building only gave access to a courtyard with no other exits. The front door was the only way in or out.

I'd seen about a dozen callers come and go within the first hour, some were known to me and some weren't. All were without doubt junkies.

The dealing went on for hours, an endless stream of people in and out of the close and still no sign of Robin or any of his family.

There must have been a good amount of heroin stashed in or about the flat as they didn't have to leave the building at any time to replenish their stocks.

If they had a 'stash' in another flat in the building it would be nigh-on impossible for me to establish where it was without more information.

I quite simply didn't have that information and there was absolutely no chance of me ever receiving it.

This tribe didn't share their secrets with too many others and the ones who did know certainly wouldn't talk to the police or even share it with fellow Caltonians as there are always loose tongues even in such a close community as the Calton.

I needed Lady Luck to smile on me for once.

Time was wearing on and my stomach complained loudly about the lack of food, I'd remembered to take all of the required equipment but had left my sandwiches, thermos flasks containing tea and soup in the police office. No doubt they would have been scoffed by one or more of my colleagues by this time. Bloody vultures!

I could smell food, the aroma of hot sausage rolls, pies and bridies was wafting upwards from the café situated below me and from the other take-away shop *'The Rumbling Tum'* known to us as the *'Grumbling bum'* across the road, it was driving me crazy. My stomach must have thought my throat had been cut.

This was Robin's fault; he would pay dearly for this.

As I said, I'm a spiteful little sod and utterly blameless in any way to my way of thinking. Everyone else is at fault.

Robin, you're getting it son.

Lady Luck was on my side today, Robin had appeared at the front door to the close, he could be seen through the glass panels in the door. I waited for him to come out onto the street but instead of doing so he entered a room to the right of the front door as I viewed it. I knew this room to be a bin-shed, it was used to store domestic refuse in large metal containers.

He was highly unlikely to be doing the housework, emptying the refuse was not going to be one of his priorities.

Going by the colour of the once white net curtains hanging from the front windows of his flat any type of housework wasn't a priority there.

This was possibly the clue I'd been hoping for. I almost said *'praying for'* but praying isn't a strong point of mine except when I'm in serious shit or giving evidence in court. These two quite often run together.

Yet more callers came and went, it was an almost never ending stream of customers and the system never altered. Press the buzzer, wait, enter, and leave after a few minutes.

There he was again at the door and not coming out onto the street. Robin entered the bin room and returned upstairs seconds later.

I had him; *'the stash'* had to be in with the garbage.

It would be somewhere in that room where no-one would come across it accidentally, it wouldn't be hidden in a bin as the Glasgow City Council Cleansing Dept may call and the stash would be lost.

It wouldn't be concealed anywhere it could be easily found but had still to be quite easily accessed.

A loose brick in the wall? A floor tile which can be lifted ? What's on the bin-shed ceiling?

I'd seen enough, time to make a quick exit.

If I could time it right and there was a lull in the activity at number 8 Bain Street, I would exit from my place of concealment, do a sharp right turn onto Gallowgate and make my way on foot back to London Road Police Office.

The filthy curtains at their front window were still closed and the street was quiet as I left. First part of the job had been completed successfully.

On my return to the office I briefed the Det/Inspector as to what I'd seen and was told, *'get the search warrant son and turn it tomorrow, I want him in the cells, I'll boot your arse if you get this wrong'*. I loved that old guy.

He would've booted my backside, but he also knew whose side I was on.

I filled in the form requesting a Justice of the Peace warrant be granted to search for controlled drugs as it was now too late for me to obtain a warrant from a Sheriff.

Trying to obtain a Sheriff's warrant was very time consuming and as it was now later in the day that was out of the question.

As it happens, I knew a J.P. who lived not a million miles from the Barras and he was only too happy to oblige and signed my warrant to search for controlled drugs. The J.P. had a large smile on his face and wished me *'good hunting Willie'*.

The Det/I. was a canny old bugger, whilst I was out at the Justice of the Peace having the paperwork attended to; he had detailed another detective to accompany me during the search and had arranged for a team of plain clothes cops to assist us.

They were simply the best, the usual suspects. Smith, Mackie, McLeod and Carrigan. The other detective on the *'turn'* was to be Henderson. What a half back line, as safe as houses.

All were in the office when I returned with the signed search warrant.

They had the same attitude as me, they trusted me and I trusted them. We had known each other for years and had no fears as to our capabilities.

We truly were The Untouchables.

I briefed the troops on what the initial information had been and saw a few knowing smiles as some of the lads deduced who the informant was.

Nothing was said, an informants identity was sacrosanct even if the buggers knew anyway.

This job was going to be *'toffee'*, I'd taken the precaution of obtaining a pass-key for the controlled entry at number 8 Bain Street from a source who shall for ever remain nameless as he/she still resides in the area.

Yes, I do have friends in low places.

We all attended at London Road Police Office at 8a.m. the following morning.

The tactics to be employed were decided amongst us as we sat in the rest room drinking tea and coffee, we all had an equal say as every one of us had loads of experience and had something of value to add.

When the boys had finished with their theories and suggestions regarding our tactics I told them how it would be done, sorry, it's not a democracy.

Yes, I am still a bastard.

This job would be done my way.

The dealing began about 10 a.m. therefore the majority of the drugs would be in place before the dealing took place. We would strike before any callers could attend there and hopefully recover the stash before any was sold.

Another alternative was to allow the transactions to take place and then detain the callers as they left the flat, but to be truthful (sorry, that word hurts, ex drugs squad, know what I mean?) we didn't have the resources to do that although it is preferable to hitting and hoping.

We would be in, through the front door of the close using the pass key donated by my friend, smash down the door to the flat before they were even out of their beds.

The lads agreed with me, *'Faither knows best'*, Quietly, quietly, for the initial approach then smash the door to the flat down and get inside quickly,. Secure every room and have every person in that flat under control before commencing a thorough search.

Bearing in mind, I already suspect where the stash is concealed, I go ahead with the raid. We never actually referred to an operation as a raid, the term used was *'a turn'*.

I love seeing the bad guy's door being splintered. If drugs are found and the property is owned by the City, the cost of repairing the door isn't borne by the taxpayer, it is borne by the bad guy himself. No flies on this old guy.

Two bites at the cherry.

He'll get whatever sentence the court passes plus the cost of replacing the door. Sounds trivial but I don't want to pay for his new door, would you?

9a.m. Thursday morning, we parked two unmarked police vehicles on Gallowgate near to Frank Mitchell's T.V. shop out of sight of the address to be searched. The street was quiet, very few people about. So far so good.

Making the rest of the journey on foot and keeping tight to the building we would not be seen from flats above.

I opened the door at the close mouth with my pass key and up the minging (dirty, smelly) stairs we go. Not a sound, these guys are good, no stage whispers, not even a cough. I am not the biggest, to be honest (that word really does haunt me) Carrigan and Mackie are by far the biggest of the bunch. They both took a run at the door which splintered and came off its hinges, we piled in.

The occupants were already standing in the hallway, Robin pulling up his jeans and his sister wearing a form of nightshirt which barely covered her naughty bits. Neither too pleased at our intrusion to say the least, but offering no resistance which was a bit of a shame because I would have loved an excuse to stick one on his chin. *'Nae gratuitous violence though'*.

I would have quite happily whacked any of them given half an excuse, Each one of that family had a face you would never have tired of punching.

The mother wasn't present and only Robin and his sister were there.

The house was absolutely filthy and stank to the heavens. No change there then!

I showed both of these creatures the warrant and cautioned them regarding their possession of any controlled substances in the flat.

They just ignored me and refused to speak. Their prerogative I suppose.

I radioed back to London Road Police Office and requested that a policewoman be despatched to 8 Bain Street in order that the sister could be searched.

I wouldn't be popular with the girl who had to attend as this would be a *'rubber gloves'* job. Still, some-one has to do it. Just glad it wasn't me. It would be nauseating enough having to search Robin.

Whilst I was giving Robin a none too gentle *'pat down'* search just to ensure he wasn't carrying anything dangerous such as a knife, razor or similar, the intercom buzzed. Donnie McLeod answered it and smiled as he said: *"Sorry the shop is shut, Robin just got the jail"*.

We heard the sound of running feet outside as the penny dropped with the potential customers and *"Oh F..k it's the polis"*.

We then systematically took the house apart, searching absolutely everywhere it was possible to look, leaving nothing untouched as we looked for the drugs. Robin had been handcuffed and looked on as his home was left tidier than we'd found it.

Whilst searching his bedroom I noticed two indentations in the dirty yellowish coloured pillows, also the bed was still warm. I made my way into the other bedroom and saw the bed hadn't been slept in and was cold.

Draw your own conclusions. I know what I thought.

Below the mattress in Robin's room, Donnie McLeod found a school jotter, *(I'm glad he lifted the mattress, I would rather have kissed Mary McKee's fat backside)* the type children used do sums in at primary school. The pages were filled with wee squares and each square would be used for one number.

I hadn't seen one of these arithmetic jotters for years. Quite a few years come to think of it.

Many of the pages had been removed and the jotter was very thin.

I asked Robin to account for it being under his mattress, he didn't even reply.

Uncivil little shit.

Normally paper from glossy magazines would be used to create folds for containing powders but in truth any paper can be used.

Two policewomen had by this time arrived to take charge of the female, I asked the taller of them if a wee peck on the cheek was out of the question, she snarled back at me. I took that to be a definite *'no'* then.

She probably didn't like boys anyway. This *'poliwumman'* could have played centre half for Baillieston Juniors. Thighs like tree trunks and a better moustache than mine. Perhaps I didn't really want that wee peck anyway.

After about an hour the search of the house was concluded and no drugs, cash or *'tick lists'* had been recovered, Robin was beginning to show signs of relaxing, he was even daring to smirk. I'd kept hold of the arithmetic jotter though.

I told Robin we would be taking him to London Road office for a full body search then I'd decide what action to take next. He shrugged his narrow shoulders as if it didn't really matter to him what I had planned and he remained silent.

As we took him and his sister down the filthy stairs towards the front door he involuntarily glanced towards the bin-shed door.

That would do for me.

I pulled him into the room and told the cretin we would have a look there before going on to the police station.

His face fell. There was suddenly a distinct smell of shit in the place and I wasn't the guilty party this time.

Detective Henderson took hold of him and along with the other cops stood at the door. The stink may have been partly responsible for that. Robin had turned paler than his usual pallor now. It wasn't a very big room and as you would expect of a place used for storing domestic garbage, it was rotten. It was perhaps about 10 feet by 10 feet and lit by three fluorescent lights on the ceiling and contained 6 metal wheelie bins filled with all sorts of rubbish. I'd search them too if necessary. I love this job...

I looked about for the loose brick or floor tile, a clue. Nothing obvious.

Looking upwards for inspiration, there it was, metal ventilation ducting suspended from the roof of the cellar. There was a gap of about six inches between the top of the duct and the roof.

Pulling a bin over, I looked at Robin, he was almost crying. This surely had to be it.

I reached into the gap and ran my right hand along the top of the duct which was filthy, coated in a thick layer of dust and grime. The paper deals were all there, lined up like wee soldiers, dozens of them all wrapped in *'arithmetic'* paper.

Got you! I detest you Robin for all of the times in the past when you ran away from me and laughed. I'm no athlete but this time you've lost the game!

Feeling quite pleased with myself now, I reminded Robin of the caution and showed him what had been recovered and asked if he wished to make any comment regarding the paper folds.

Still not a word passed his lips.

One of the *'plainers'*, I think it was Mackie, handed me an A4 sized clear polythene bag and I placed the *'deals'* very carefully inside, I would require to have the paper wrappings examined for fingerprint impressions.

The wrappings would also be compared to the remaining pages in the jotter to ascertain if they were from the same source.

Even if Robin hadn't bagged the heroin himself I could still find out who had. Things were looking bad for him and I was the one smirking now. There were about 100 £10 bags stashed on top of the duct.

Not a bad result, I would settle for that.

Next stop was London Road office for a full body search and tape recorded interview.

If Robin thought he was having a bad day, it just got worse. The bar-officer who was conducting the body search which was being witnessed by me reached into a tight *'ticket pocket'* in Robins denim jeans and found another two £10 bags which Robin had obviously forgotten about. They were of course wrapped in the same squared arithmetic paper.

A real bonus. This was game set and match to the polis.

Robin just stared glumly at the floor, his world was at an end.

I had him detained for an appearance at Glasgow Sheriff Court the following day and asked that he be refused bail.

His sister had been searched and was released without charge; I would have struggled to prove anything regarding her involvement in the drugs trafficking. She was as guilty as sin but knowing it and proving it are not the same thing.

However, her mother might just learn about her son and daughter sharing a bed.

There is more than one way to skin a cat.

I went for my weekend-off fully expecting to find a request from the Fiscal's Office for full statements in the case against Robin on my desk when I returned for my night shift the following Monday.

A week passed by and nothing was received, this was very unusual, I was in the horrors, had I made a mistake and the case had been thrown out.

The grumpy Det/Inspector would slay me.

He would ask me what the result had been. I could always lie!!!

When I was a very young detective, a Det/Chief Inspector had given me a piece of very valuable advice which I may soon have to fall back on. He said, *'Lie when cornered son'*

Boot my backside? I would be pulling padlocks for the rest of my career.

I contacted a friend of mine, John D, who worked in the Fiscal's Office in Ballater Street in Glasgow and asked him to find out what had happened to my drugs case.

John, who is an ardent fan of Glasgow Celtic football club and had suffered a lot of verbal punishment from me during Rangers nine league title wins in a row called me back a short time later.

"Willie what have you done? The Regional Fiscal is writing to the Chief Constable about you. You're in deep shit this time".

After a few seconds of silence in which I was mentally preparing my escape route for when the D/I would demand an answer for his boss, John relented and said: *"Your man got two years in the jail; he pleaded guilty on his lawyers advice last Monday'".*

And I thought I was a bastard?

The world turns slowly, I'll see John D again some day.

I passed by the flat at number 8 Bain Street in the Calton fairly recently, the same filthy curtains are still hanging at the windows.

My pal Frankie

I liked Frankie Nolan; he was a thief, a bit of a housebreaker at times and a heroin addict who would abuse almost any other type of drugs when he couldn't lay his dirty mitts on a tenner bag of smack.

I can name Frankie because he is long dead, having departed this world thanks to an inevitable overdose of a Class 'A' drug contaminated with brick dust.

I'd locked him up on many an occasion for his thieving activities going back to when I was a uniformed cop pounding my beat in the Duke Street area of Glasgow and he was still only a teenager. Frankie was actually quite a likeable rogue and such an inept felon that he would be caught for practically every crime he committed. Inept or just plain unlucky, I really don't know.

One saving grace was his habit of never going to trial with anything he'd been charged with; he would change his not guilty plea to one of guilty just before the trial commenced, quite often resulting in me receiving an overtime payment of five and a half hours at day off rate.

He wasn't all bad.

I hasten to add, this was not an arrangement between Frankie Nolan and myself; it was simply what he did. If he adhered to his not guilty plea until the day of the trial then he would stay out of prison for a wee bit longer. He was only delaying the inevitable. A plea of guilty would be entered by his solicitor on the day and invariably that plea would be accepted by the Crown No trial was then required and Frankie would receive a lighter sentence as a result.

Bluevale Street & Whitevale Street flats

The boy wasn't totally stupid. Neither was his lawyer who still had to be paid quite handsomely from the public purse through the Legal Aid scheme for simply attending the Glasgow Sheriff Court and going through the motions of entering a plea and telling the Court that his client had been forced into a life of crime to feed his drugs habit but was hoping to start a job on Monday, etc., etc., etc.

Frankie hadn't worked a day in his short life and if he could help it, never would.

He lived with his mother, father, sister and younger brother Des in a maisonette flat in Bluevale Street, Dennistoun.

The parents were decent enough people but Frankie and Des (Derek) grew up in a culture of thieving and drugs abuse amongst their peers. They had absolutely no chance of keeping that pair in check given the company the boys were exposed to.

The block of flats they lived in is about halfway down the hill, midway between Duke Street and Gallowgate and overlooks a pedestrian concourse which itself separates two blocks of multi-storey flats. As I recall, these tower blocks at 51 Whitevale Street and 109 Bluevale Street are twenty-six floors high and are occupied by a huge cross section of humanity. Everything from decent ordinary couples, pensioners, single people, *'refugees'* from the Barrowfield, Calton and Bridgeton along with the homeless who were often housed there by Glasgow City Council to keep them off the street and out of the city's hostels.

A real mixture.

One day, not long before Christmas, Frankie looked out from his living-room window onto the pedestrian area between the two multi-storey blocks which had a dusting of snow covering it.

He watched as two people, a male and a female, walked from 109 Bluevale Street, which was to his left, towards 51 Whitevale Street which was located to his right.

He recognised them as being from the nearby Calton district and knew then to be junkies and thieving housebreakers; not unlike himself.

Both were carrying heavy looking holdall bags and the male was struggling to drag a large wheeled suitcase behind him.

Instead of heading along Comleypark Street towards Calton, the couple entered through the front door at 51 Whitevale Street.

Frankie, being a thief himself, suspected they had been up to no good.

About ten minutes later, the pair re-appeared from the multi-storey and made their way back across the pedestrian area to the other block and entered through that front door.

My pal Frankie smelled a rat.

Sure enough, about ten minutes later, they emerged from the block carrying a number of cardboard boxes and plastic carrier bags.

I was sitting at my desk in London Road police office, looking out of the window at the falling snow and idly wondering what the road conditions up to East Kilbride and home would be like. If it snowed in Glasgow my home town would be like the Arctic. Suddenly the phone on my desk rang and I was awake again.

It was Frankie.

"Wullie, ah've jist seen S.L. and his burd; ah think they've tanned a house in the Bluevale Street flats".

He never referred to me by my title; I always insisted the neds called me *'Mr Greenshields'* or *'Mr Greenshields, Sir'* but Frankie just called me Wullie anyway.

He went on to recount what he'd seen and I had to agree with his assessment of the situation. I felt he was probably spot-on and said I'd get back to him later. I asked him to keep watching out for S.L. and his lady friend.

He would do that for me.

No sooner was he off the phone than I was on it again. A quick call to the caretaker's office at 51 Whitevale Street to ask if either S.L. or his *'burd'* had been allocated a flat there.

"Yes" was the immediate reply; they had moved into a flat on the eighth floor about a month before and had already been the subject of complaints from neighbours because of noise and callers to the flat at all hours of the day and night.

I made my way to the warrants office which was located on the top floor of the police office. This was manned by two older cops, Roy and Alec. (my snooker opponents every lunchtime)

They had a rummage through their files and handed me a copy of an arrest warrant, not for S.L. but for his girlfriend. That would do nicely.

I could now legitimately boot their door down and you never know what I might accidentally stumble upon there.

The long-suffering D/C St...n was press ganged into action once again; this poor sod must have cringed every time I looked at or spoke to him.

I phoned Frankie and was told that neither of the felons had reappeared on the street; they were more than likely still in their flat.

I then phoned the caretaker who said that, as far as he was aware, they hadn't left the building.

I requested the assistance of the beat cop for the area and arranged to meet him in the caretaker's office; he was probably there anyway as it was a haunt for the beat cops. It had an electric fire, comfortable easy chairs, radio, television and a kettle. I know because I used to be the beat cop there. Happy days indeed!

We arrived at the block before ten minutes had elapsed, collected our uniformed colleague as arranged and made our way via the lift to the eighth floor.

If they were still at home, there was no way out for them unless they wanted to jump from the balcony. What a nice thought!

Knocking loudly on the front door with a feather duster, I received no response from within but could hear male and female voices in conversation.

No time to waste; they could dispose of any property held there by lobbing it out of the window. I really didn't want that to happen.

The uniformed cop, who was a big lump of a boy, almost took the front door off its hinges with one kick.

In we went; straight into the living-room which was on the right at the end of a short hallway.

S.L. was getting to his feet and the girl was sitting on the floor surrounded by Christmas presents still in their boxes. Pots, pans, crockery, cutlery and photograph frames still containing sepia coloured images of people dressed in clothing from the early 1900's. They had even taken this person's Christmas cards.

This pair had been furnishing their flat by using the contents of an old lady's home.

The victim's bank books and pension books were also recovered there.

There would be no difficulty in identifying where it had all come from.

Two uniformed cops were despatched to the address we now knew about and, shortly thereafter, called me to say the old lady's flat had just been ransacked.

These cretins would be *'getting the jail'*. I love Glasgow terminology.

I noticed the female was wearing lots of jewellery on her fingers and around her neck. I would have that too.

S.L. was his usual aggressive self, snarling at us and at me in particular. He'd hated the sight of me ever since my early days as a uniformed cop walking the beat in the Calton and the Barras.

I'd caused him a lot of grief back then and he'd done a bit of time because of me. I'd locked him up for breaking into shops at the bottom end of London Road and Gallowgate near to Glasgow Cross on more than one occasion.

There was no love lost between us. The feeling was mutual. Absolute hatred.

I've often said that some criminals are bearable, some even quite likeable, but this reprobate had no good points.

I really wanted him to have a go at me physically; any excuse to plant one on his chin would do for me. It is a failing in my character, but I like it.

He obviously sensed what was going through my head and backed off.

Shame about that, but there would be no gratuitous violence; he would have no cause to complain about my conduct.

The caretaker at the other block would have to be alerted as to which flat had been the subject of the break-in so as to prepare the old lady for the shock awaiting her at home. She would have to be intercepted in the hallway prior to entering the lift. I didn't want the old dear to stumble into an almost empty flat ignorant of the fact that we had already the thieves and had hopefully recovered everything they had stolen from her.

Having arranged transport for the two prisoners and the property back to the police office, I handcuffed the male and female before escorting them down in the lift to the pedestrian area where the police vehicle would be waiting.

No doubt Frankie would be too.

Sure enough, there he was, half-concealed behind his living-room curtain, grinning from ear to ear.

He had no time for S.L. either.

I had also arranged for a Scenes of Crimes officer to attend at London Road office to photograph the recovered property which I could then return to the old lady's flat. I would, thereafter, have him conduct a fingerprint examination of the flat which had been violated.

It may seem to be a bit of a belt and braces job but knowing S.L. of old, he would fight me all the way and contest everything tooth and nail.

He'd been jailed before and would not be looking forward to going back inside and to make matters worse, it was me who had jailed him again.

Both S.L. and his girlfriend were detained for an appearance at Glasgow Sheriff Court the following day.

She pleaded guilty to the charge of committing a theft by housebreaking and was sentenced to six months in Cornton Vale Woman's Prison in Stirling. A smart move on her lawyer's part to advise her to admit her guilt, as she was going there anyway due to the existence of the arrest warrant which was of the 'go directly to jail, do not pass Go' type.

There would have been no sense in her pleading 'not guilty' and then spending a few months in prison before receiving another six months sentence when she could do it all at one time.

S.L. on the other hand adhered to his 'not guilty' plea as I'd fully expected him to do. He did not however walk free, but was instead remanded in custody to await trial.

At least he could now be sure of having a turkey dinner to follow his lumpy porridge.

As expected, he went the distance and eventually stood trial at Glasgow Sheriff Court on a miserable wet Thursday afternoon early in January, which just so happened to be my rest day. I was earning yet another five and a half hours of overtime which was payable at the enhanced day off rate.

Thanks again Frankie boy.

S.L.'s lawyer, his defence agent claimed that his client had merely found the property within the Bluevale Street multi-storey and as he required to furnish his new flat, it would come in very handy.

Just one wee problem; the Scenes of Crimes officer had indeed recovered fingerprint impressions belonging to the accused inside the old lady's flat. The prints had been found on the mirrored door of a medicine cabinet within her bathroom. What type of drugs would they've been looking for in an old ladies toilet?

His Lordship, the Sheriff, wasn't impressed with S.L.'s alibi and I was a bit surprised not to have been accused of having planted the fingerprint impressions for the Scenes of Crimes guy to find. I've been down that road before.

That was the norm. When it is all going wrong; allege the cop has fitted up the accused.

I would dearly love to see a lawyer getting done for that because they are knowingly telling lies to the Court. Of course, it will never happen.

It's all part of the game, Judges were once lawyers too. They all belong to the same club and in my opinion will protect each other no matter what.

The tale entitled 'The Jeweller' in 'Greenshields - A Glasgow Cop', my first book, is a perfect example of lawyers protecting their own kind. After all these years that travesty still rankles a bit with me. But I'm not bitter...

No fit-up, no miscarriage of justice and 15 months in the jail to further seethe with hatred at the very thought of me.

Still, S.L. would have a few of my victims to share his thoughts with in the 'big hoose', Barlinnie prison in Glasgow. Take my advice son; don't drop the soap in the showers!

Frankie's family moved to Galston in Ayrshire soon afterwards. His parents thought that moving away from Glasgow would prevent young Frankie from sourcing and using controlled drugs.

As if moving to another part of the country would make the slightest bit of difference.

The poor boy was dead within a year but I dare say the number of thefts by housebreaking in that part of Ayrshire had declined sharply too.

Cynical? No. I'm quite simply a realist.

Frankie – there's more!

Night shift with Detective Sergeant Jim F was always easy on me, Jim, known as Felty was so competent and laid-back that I was never under any pressure to make the hard decisions when problems sometimes cropped up.

He was about the same age as me but had a bit more service and a lot less hair, we got on well together, his snooker skills were also on a par with mine, poor bordering on rubbish.

Monday night was usually a quiet start to the night shift so I was a bit surprised to hear a call on the police radio to the effect that an alarm had been activated in the Overdale Bar which is located at the corner of Hunter Street and Duke Street.

It was a silent alarm and it had registered at the office of a private security company who in turn contacted the police

If there was indeed an intruder within the premises he would be unaware that the alarm was in operation.

Felty and I pulled on our jackets and hurried from office, I almost claimed to have run but that was never the case with me. We got into our state of the art, drab, brown coloured Austin Maestro which was parked in the back yard of the police station. If you weren't careful when shifting the gear lever, it would come out of its socket and you'd be left holding a disconnected, useless piece of metal in your left hand. It had happened on quite a few occasions previously.

The uniformed cops starting their night shift would still be *'mustering'* within the police office and the late-shift would be off duty so the chances of there being any police officers on the street at that time was very unlikely. Indeed it was the ideal time to commit a crime. Felty informed the control-room staff that he and I would attend at the pub and thereafter assess the situation.

The Overdale Bar is situated on the ground and first floor of a four storey tenement block, there is a public bar and a lounge bar on the ground floor with a further lounge and function suite on the upper floor.

A friend of mine, a former taxi-driver, big Robert F was the pub manager. We went back a long way, but that's another story.

Overdale Bar

It would be advisable for us to get to the pub before he did, if there was a housebreaker within, Robert would be less than pleased and the Casualty Dept at the nearby Glasgow Royal Infirmary would certainly have another customer in need of emergency treatment. Robert was a big boy with a very short fuse.

Felty turned off the Maestro's engine and cruised silently downhill from Sydney Street to a spot on Duke Street about twenty yards away from the front door of the pub where he stopped the car. There were no flies on Felty.

We closed the car doors carefully and approached very quietly on foot; I tried the front door of the pub which was found to be secure and walked around the corner onto Hunter Street.

Surprise, surprise, who did I find crouching on a window ledge which was about six feet off the ground, Frankie.

He had his right arm inside the open hopper window and was receiving a bottle of whisky from an accomplice who was inside the bar.

There were another dozen or so bottles of various spirits lined up alongside the wall of the building, Frankie and his mate must been there for some time and being blissfully unaware they had triggered the alarm via a motion censor continued to steal whatever they could lay their hands on.

The look on his face was a joy to behold when he saw us standing a few feet away from him.

"Aw f..k, no you Wullie".

I replied: *"Aye Frankie, it's jail time".*

Never one to give me any bother, he just slid down from his roost and allowed me to put the cuffs on him. Why can't they all be like that?

Our uniformed colleagues were now on the scene as was a very irate pub manager, big Robert.

Frank was safely ensconced in the rear of our car when Robert arrived, I liked Frank and would not have willingly sacrificed him to Robert's wrath.

There was however the probability that there was at least one person still within the pub, Felty asked Robert to unlock the front door and let our colleagues inside, Robert would have to wait outside meantime.

It wouldn't look too good in our written report to the boss in the morning if we had to tell him we'd caught the thief only for the bar-manager to seriously assault him or God forbid, even worse. Robert was a monster.

There was no sign of the pub having been broken into and the hopper window was too small for anyone to have climbed in through.

At first the troops failed to find anyone in the pub which had been ransacked but when Felty suggested in a stage whisper that we let Robert inside to assist with the search, a panel in the false ceiling very quickly began to move and the ugly face of Stuart G a known accomplice and near neighbour of Frankies' appeared.

He hadn't broken into the premises but had in fact climbed into a space above the false ceiling in the Gents toilet shortly before closing time and waited until Robert had locked up before emerging into the now empty premises.

The bold Frankie was waiting outside for Stuart to open the window onto Hunter Street and hand him the spoils.

Stuart would then have to squeeze himself out of the window to escape. Being as thin as a rake there wouldn't have been a great problem.

A cunning plan except for the fact this pair of inept *'burglars'* didn't notice the motion censors positioned around interior walls of the pub premises.

Our uniformed colleagues could now deal with this, Felty and I would no doubt return to the office to have a frame or two of snooker.

The uniformed shift inspector (a man I absolutely despise even to this day, he gets his first mention on page 20 of book 1) had also turned up, possibly because it was a pub that had been the subject of the crime and there may have been a small reward offered to the troops by the manager, call me a cynic !

The Inspector told his cops to charge Frankie and his mate Stuart with theft by housebreaking

Felty shook his head, this was never a theft by housebreaking, nothing had been broken into.

This pair had conspired together to commit the common law crime of theft.

The Inspector wasn't best pleased to get it wrong and then to be corrected in front of his troops. At least Felty knew his *'Definitions'* even if the Inspector did not.

He was also disappointed not to be rewarded by the manager, my pal Robert.

Felty and I were already in possession of the prize.

We would no doubt have a wee nightcap at the end of our shift.

Millroad Drive

Don't take a fence

The Calton was without doubt a tough part of the city of Glasgow, it had its own gang known as the *'Calton Tongs'* and wasn't a place particularly amenable to strangers.

Like every other place though, decent people lived there too, but there will always be the element that will not conform to living a normal life and are beyond redemption.

They will prey on anyone whether they be strangers or neighbours.

Not long before I left the *'East'* I'd been night-shift with another detective who was slightly older than me and had been away from the division for many years. He had, I believe, served in the Drugs Squad for about twelve years before returning to the *'East'*.

A thoroughly decent man, if a bit nervous at times.

I'd fallen out with the female officer I'd been partnered with over my taking part in a drugs raid on a house in Slatefield Street in the Gallowgate without telling her where I was going.

She really took umbrage at me because I could think for myself whilst she was somewhere else in the city doing her shopping. We were never on speaking terms again after that, good, that would suit me. Knit one, purl one, drink of diet Coke, knit one, purl one, drink of diet Coke. Her idea of policing and mine were poles apart and always will be.

The Detective Superintendent who was near to retiring rewarded me with a new partner, Joe C and we were soon working the night shift together.

It was a quiet Monday night, the first night on that particular shift; Joe and I were having a drive about our sub-division before heading back into London Road office for a cup of coffee and a few frames of snooker before the uniformed guys came in for their breaks. No change there then.

We would vacate the snooker room until they were all back out on the street then go in for a few more frames if all was still quiet.

Life can be tough in the trenches.

Our snooker playing abilities did improve after a week on nights.

The control room staff always knew where to find us and didn't have to call us on the radio very often, they either phoned the C.I.D. general office or the snooker room.

The pubs had spilled their remaining clients about midnight and nothing which required C.I.D. attention had occurred.

Give it another hour or so and we could relax for the rest of the shift.

My snooker cue was propped against the wall next to my desk and I could almost smell the coffee brewing. It smelled better than it tasted.

As we drove along Gallowgate near to its junction with Fielden Street, Jo and I heard a sound neither of us wanted to hear. An ambulance siren, it was becoming louder, getting closer to us.

I rolled down the car window and listened, it wasn't far away.

Maybe it's an accident or a sudden illness, I thought.

Sods law, the local police radio burst into life, the control room were looking for us urgently.

We already had the feeling it was going to be a long night, my snooker cue may not see the blue chalk for a while.

We'd to make our way with all speed to Millroad Drive in the Calton as a young man had been seriously assaulted and suffered a severe facial injury as he and his younger brother were walking home from a closed door session in a local pub.

We arrived in time to see the ambulance crew lifting a man onto a stretcher and into the rear of the vehicle.

My first impression of the scene was of the amount of blood on the road and footway; this must be quite an injury to the young guy's face.

His brother had made off successfully from the scene without any injury and reached the safety of his home where he'd caused their mother to summon the police and an ambulance.

Taking the younger brother to one side, we asked him what had happened and did he know who had assaulted the older brother.

His reply was evasive and not very forthcoming.

It was quite obvious to my partner and I that the boy was holding information back from us.

The story he gave was along the lines of, he and his brother had been in the Squirrel bar down at the Barras until well after closing time. This was not unusual as they were locals and never caused any trouble in the pub.

Sometime about 12:30 a.m. they decided to call it a day and walk home the short distance along Stevenson Street towards the Calton.

Having drunk too many pints than was good for them, it's not advisable to drink on an empty head; the brothers were singing 'Irish Rebel' songs at the tops of their voices as they neared Millroad Drive. Not a very sensible idea in that particular part of the Calton.

They both suddenly heard the sound of running feet coming up behind them and on looking back saw a group of youths sprinting towards them all carrying large sticks. A real brown trousers moment.

Fearing for their safety, both did the wise thing and ran off towards home which was close-by.

The younger brother got away safely; his older and more heavily built brother did not.

On looking back, the younger sibling saw this group of youths standing over the prone figure of his brother on the ground whilst pummelling him with their long sticks.

I looked about for what potentially may have been a weapon used against the young man.

I found it lying nearby at the side of the road, a piece of chestnut fencing with dark staining at it's rather blunt tapered end.

Being no expert, the staining appeared to me at any rate to be blood.

Showing it to my reluctant witness, I asked: *"Could this be one of the sticks you referred to"*. He shrugged his shoulders and said: *"Aye mibbe"*.

I retained the *'stick'* for forensic examination.

We hadn't even been to the Glasgow Royal Infirmary yet to check on the condition of the victim; that would have to be our next port of call.

Thankfully the Casualty Department there was quiet that morning, it is the busiest Casualty Department in Europe apparently and the medical staff have little or no time to spare to talk to the police.

On approaching the wee red haired nursing sister in charge of that department, a nippy sweetie, to ask where I could locate the boy, I didn't even have to speak; she merely pointed to a cubicle and said, *'in there'*. (I would come across her again later in my career when as a Drugs Squad officer suffering from a war wound, a broken finger suffered when struggling with a drugs dealer who was reluctant to see the inside of a police cell, she had pinned a tin badge onto my jacket which read, *'I've been a brave boy at the doctor's today'*. Cheeky wee bugger.)

Inside the cubicle a nurse was standing over the victim who was lying face up on a trolley; she was busily cleaning what I can only describe as being the worst facial injury I've ever seen. There was a gaping ragged hole where his left cheek should have been.

The nurse said it appeared that a blunt instrument had been forced through his cheek and into the mouth causing immense trauma to both.

The interior of his mouth had been almost destroyed.

To my mind this incident was no longer an assault to severe injury but would be treated as an attempted murder.

This boy wouldn't be able to help with my enquiries for quite some time.

We would have to go back to the locus and speak with the brother, I felt he knew exactly who had done this awful thing to his older sibling and for whatever reason wouldn't speak up.

It had to be fear. He was from a Catholic family and along with his older brother had been singing Irish rebel songs when they'd been set upon by a gang of youths. It wasn't rocket science to work out who the suspects were.

The other Calton faction.

We attended at the family home which is only about 40 yards away from where the assault had occurred and were admitted to the mid-terraced house by a woman in her housecoat who would probably have been in her mid to late forties. She was the mother.

Again I asked the younger brother what had happened and who were the assailants.

He adhered to his story about being chased by unknown youths and I pressed him again to tell me who they were. He must have known them, no-one wanders around the Calton at night in a group if they don't belong there.

Locals were responsible for this deed; there was no doubt in my mind about that. This guy was really too scared to talk.

It was by now far too late to go knocking on peoples doors looking for witnesses.

I wanted this enquiry for myself, a bit greedy and even more selfish, but what the hell.

I waited for the ill tempered Det/Inspector coming on duty in the morning, he came into the office about 07:30 a.m. as was his habit. My eyes were burning with tiredness and I wanted to get home to bed but I didn't want to let go of this one. He always scowled as he entered the general office. Are senior officers taught to do that or does it just come naturally? Torn faced old sod.

I related the story to him and asked that I be allocated the enquiry.

He was only too happy to be shot of it and I was told get on with it.

My only other request to him was that I be allowed to start work at 7p.m. that day instead of 11p.m. in order that I could knock on doors where the incident occurred in an effort to drum up a witness or two.

The usual deal; Get *'a body'* for this and the overtime payment would be authorised.

Miserable old bastard!

Still, I had the enquiry now, that was half the battle.

After coming back on duty later that day I called at the victim's home where I found the brother, he very reluctantly emerged from his bedroom and wasn't at all pleased to see me. We sat in the kitchen drinking tea whilst I noted a statement from him regarding the previous night's events. He wasn't for budging one inch as to the identities of the assailants so I called his mother into the kitchen and told her that her son knew who had committed this dreadful assault but wouldn't tell me their names. He sat silently; head bowed and didn't deny it.

I left them alone for a few minutes and sat in the living-room drinking another cup of tea to await the result of their conversation.

His mother came into the living-room shaking her head. The boy was adamant. Under no circumstances would he tell me anything about who had been responsible for this atrocity. He was terrified of the inevitable repercussions if he spoke to the police. She was unable to persuade him to speak up.

I would like to have taken him back to the police office and had a very private word in his ear but I think his mother would suspect what my intentions were. No way would she permit me to be left alone with her son in a police office.

I'd have another go at him later, this enquiry would take a bit of time and I had lots of that. Patience is a virtue.

I made my way around the houses knocking on doors and asking the obvious questions. Did you or any other occupant hear or see anything occur outside in the street not long after midnight last night?

All deaf and blind, I was beginning to despair and trying to think up another strategy, when there is payment for four hours overtime at stake I would not give up easily. Altruistic I am not.

One last house to try in Millroad Drive. The door was opened by Mrs Mac, a small wizened woman who was probably only about fifty years of age. I asked her the same questions I'd asked her neighbours.

'Aye son' was the wonderful reply.

She and her profoundly deaf husband (genuinely deaf, not Calton deaf) had been watching a film on T.V. (I wondered if it had sub-titles?) when she heard the sound of shouting coming from the street outside her home.

Being a very nosey wee woman she just had to have a look to find out what was going on.

Mrs Mac told me she had seen two boys being chased by another group of about four or five people who were doing the shouting, they were all running from the direction of Millroad Street along Millroad Drive when one of the two being chased fell onto the roadway and was immediately set upon by the pursuing pack, two of whom were armed with long wooden sticks.

She went on to say the members of the mob were kicking the boy who was lying on the ground and one of the pursuers was striking him on the head with a stick.

Did she know who these people were?

"Aye son J.F. and his brother A.F. were the ones with the sticks, their fat pal, I don't know his name , the one who is always with them, you know who I mean and somebody I've never seen before".

The fat one was *'fat Andy'* I'd had some dealings with him previously and certainly knew the F. family, they were from Millroad Street. An entire family of drugs dealers, robbers and thieves.

If you'd seen one, you'd seen them all; they all had the same face.

It fitted perfectly, the two boys on their way home from the Squirrel Bar full of beer would've had to pass by the F. familys home to get to Millroad Drive and the singing of Irish rebel songs wouldn't have gone down very well with that team.

I asked the lady if she would speak up in court regarding what she'd seen and heard. *'Aye son'* was her reply.

A case would be reported to the Fiscal at some point, there was no doubt about that now and I would have my overtime payment.

I sat with the lady for over an hour and noted her statement in my notebook; it was good, very comprehensive. She read it over and quite happily signed it when asked to do so by me.

Even if she did go back on her statement now, I could produce the signed copy if necessary.

The ball was firmly in my court now.

I returned to the victims mothers house and had another go at the younger brother. I tried to pressurise him into speaking up by letting him know I was aware of the assailants' identity now.

He still refused to assist me, I even tried the emotional blackmail bit by hitting him with: *"They did this to your brother and you're letting them get away with it!"*

No, he wasn't for helping in any way; I'd have to do it without him.

The victim was still in no shape to be interviewed, I'd simply have to wait until he was fit enough to be seen.

The enquiry was put onto the back-burner for the time being; just as well I'm a very patient man.

I sought out the grumpy old D/I and told him what the state of play now was.

He would doubtless go straight to the Det/Superintendent to let him know an arrest was imminent.

All I had to do was wait for the *'complainer'* to recover sufficiently in order that I could interview him.

About a month had passed by when I learnt that the victim had been released from hospital and was now at home he and wished to see me.

My partner and I called at his home one Saturday afternoon; the young man was propped up in an armchair watching the horse-racing on T.V.

His left cheek was a mass of stitches and still bore all the colours of the rainbow due to the amount of bruising suffered. He would without doubt be scarred for life.

His speech was slurred and slow, (a bit like mine late on a Saturday night).

I asked why he wished to talk to me and was a bit surprised to hear he wished to make a statement regarding the identity of his attackers.

It was basically what his younger brother had said except he had recognised one of the pursuers as being J.F. He hadn't seen the faces of the others but J.F. was the one who did the damage to his face with the fence post.

I again took the precaution of noting his statement in my notebook and had him sign it.

I returned to my desk and put pen to paper.

The case against J.F. was prepared that day and sent off to the Fiscal's office the following Monday.

Meantime the result of the Forensic examination had come back from the police Forensic Laboratory. The blood staining on the chestnut fencing had come from the victim. I contacted the Fiscal's office again and updated them with the new information.

A week later I was told to attend at that office to collect a Warrant for the arrest of J.F.

I was to arrange to hold an Identification Parade at London Road police office in respect of J.F. and it was to be viewed by two people, the victim and the female witness, Mrs Mac.

If they successfully picked him out from the line-up then I could charge him with assault to severe injury and permanent disfigurement.

I had hoped for an attempted murder charge but the Fiscal decreed otherwise, perhaps I was chancing my arm just a wee bit, but you've got to try.

With great pleasure I assembled a *'posse'* of the usual suspects, the plain-clothes team and myself. We swooped on the F. family home in Millroad Street, normally their front door would be lying open and any number of acolytes would be milling around in the front garden. This time the door was closed, a most unusual occurrence. We immediately secured the back and front doors. No-one would be leaving the house unless we said so.

After much shouting and swearing, mostly from us, the front door was opened by the father (now, happily from my point of view, deceased).

He was an evil little man, slightly built and greying on top, with a face like a twelve year old wasp, the self styled Godfather of his large criminal family.

We didn't wait to be invited into the house. Half a dozen burly cops and I (a scrawny wimp) entered without ceremony. I did tell the *'patriarch'* that I was in possession of a warrant as I shoved him out of my way. We found J.F. sitting in the living room watching the T.V. as though nothing was amiss. His brother A.F. was standing near to the kitchen door trying to blend in with the wallpaper. He would have been expecting to be arrested too. Unfortunately not this time.

J.F. looked up as we entered the room and turned his head back to watch the telly.

He would miss the end of his programme which would not have been Mastermind or University Challenge.

I told him why we were there, as if he didn't already know and showed him the warrant for his arrest.

I did all the right things like cautioning him and asking if he had anything to say. Not a word from him. He stood up, reached over to a chair to retrieve a jacket which was lying across its back. One of the plainers got there first and took possession of the item of clothing. J.F. was a bit of a fox and may have had a weapon concealed in the jacket. Nothing was found but better safe than sorry.

I was a handsome devil and J.F. would not be allowed to spoil my Adonis like appearance. The other cops were all ugly brutes and any alterations to their faces would have been an improvement.

We bundled our prisoner out of the front door, along the *'garden'* path to the waiting unmarked C.I.D. cars. I'd taken the precaution of leaving one of the plain-clothes team with the cars. I didn't want to come back to a car with no windows or slashed tyres. This was *'bandit country'* and it wasn't unheard of to have police vehicles vandalised in this area after having being left unattended.

He was driven to London Road police office where I read the warrant over to him under tape recorded conditions.

J.F. only confirmed his name, address and date of birth to me on the tape and refused to speak further.

That actually suited me as I would have to transcribe the tape later for transmission to the Fiscal's office where it could be added to the case papers.

The less that was said on the tape the sooner I could get that tedious job done.

The fact he wasn't denying anything wasn't lost on me either.

Not unexpectedly, within about thirty minutes of J.F. being detained his lawyer had turned up at the front desk at the police office demanding access to his client. Too late, I'd anticipated his arrival and conducted the taped interview before he could get to our office.

I have an inborn dislike of criminal lawyers, it is perhaps best to leave the rest unsaid, except for this;

Question: What would you call the sinking of a ship with a thousand lawyers on board?

Answer: A very good start.

The prisoner appeared at Glasgow Sheriff Court the following day and although his lawyer requested he be bailed, the request was denied and J.F. was remanded in custody to await trial.

Police officers are not permitted to enter the court when pleading diets are being held so I don't know on what grounds bail was refused, I'm just happy he was locked up.

I could now get on with organising the Identification Parade knowing he would definitely be there without having to search the East End of the city trying to find him. He wouldn't have made himself available voluntarily.

The *'parade'* was organised for three days later, I could take no part in the running of the parade as I was the reporting officer but did organise the stand-ins etc.

All I had to do was walk round to Broad Street hostel and fight off the hoards of volunteers and pick the six who would reasonably resemble the accused and later be paid £5 or £6 for their time. If I'd had my way the stand-ins would all have been of black or Asian appearance. My appreciation of *'fairness to the accused'* may differ from some others. My sympathies will always lie with the victim.

I had seen the injuries which had been inflicted on the young man's face.

I collected Mrs Mac and the victim from home and drove them to the police office making sure they didn't come into contact at any time with the stand-ins before the *'parade'* took place.

My part in the enquiry was almost done and I took a back seat.

It was time for a coffee and a look at my Glasgow Herald crossword. (I still struggled with it, the coffee that is, not the crossword)

About an hour had passed by when one of the two detectives who were running the parade on my behalf came into the C.I.D general office; he gave me the thumbs up and held up two fingers. He was either being rude or we had two successful idents.

It couldn't have been otherwise unless one of the witnesses backed out at the last minute.

Both witnesses had picked out the accused from the line up.

Job done.

I made my way through the building to the uniform bar area where the cells are located, I wanted him to see me as he was being readied for his return trip to *'the big hoose'* Barlinnie Prison to await the trial.

J. F. was already standing there, collecting his bits and pieces from the bar officer when he saw me approaching. His face darkened and I was called a bastard.

I smiled and replied: *"don't take a fence son"*.

There were a few sniggers as he was led out to the waiting police vehicle.

Quite surprisingly there were no reprisals taken against the victim or Mrs Mac.

I had told them to let me know immediately if there was any bother but not one thing occurred to upset either one of them or members of their families.

The F family were very quiet, their front door which normally lay open was now more often than not firmly closed and the hangers-on were nowhere to be seen.

Fat Andy who was to be seen sitting on the front doorstep so often he could have been charged rent for it had disappeared off the scene entirely.

I later learned from a *'confidential source'* that the other man present when the assault took place was Hector S.... from Airdrie, I couldn't prove anything against him, more's the pity. He went on to become a serial rapist and the last I heard of him, he was serving a term of Life Imprisonment.

The day of J.F's trial duly came around; it was scheduled to be heard by a Sheriff sitting with a Jury because of the seriousness of the charge.

Mrs Mac was there, sitting in the witness room and taking it all in her stride, she was itching to take the stand and tell the world what she had seen in the street outside her home.

The victim was also in the witness room, he was sitting with his mother and brother. They were quiet, saying very little to each other. The younger brother wouldn't look at me; he averted his eyes when I looked at him. I must admit I did it intentionally as I still thought he should be thoroughly ashamed of himself. Perhaps he was.

The trial started about 11:00 a.m. with the forensics people from Police Headquarters and medical staff from Glasgow Royal Infirmary being called to give their evidence first.

The victim was the next person on the witness list; he took the stand just before mid-day and was still there when the court broke for lunch at 1p.m.

He resumed giving his evidence when the court business restarted at 2p.m. and was only released about 3.30 p.m. He must have received a torrid time from the defence as he looked shellshocked when he emerged from the court to collect his mother and brother from the waiting room.

I detest defence agents. Bloodsucking leeches.

Mrs Mac entered the fray, I thought the defence team would perhaps have a fight on their hands now; she was a totally different kettle of fish from the victim. This lady was fearless.

I would not like to have taken an open pay packet home to her.

At 4.30 p.m. the court usher emerged from the court and discharged the two cops who had run the Identification Parade, they would not now be required as both civilian witnesses had positively identified J.F. as being the man responsible for the deed.

Myself and my partner Joe.C. were told to return to the court the following day for 9.45 a.m. without fail and that I would more than likely be the first witness.

I would not be losing any sleep over this court appearance.

There have been times I must admit when attending court was a great laxative.

Not this time.

I made sure my head was clear and didn't even have a glass of wine with dinner the night before the trial restarted. There's a first time for everything.

I was sitting in the witness room along with my partner about 10a.m. when the court usher emerged from the court and stuck his head into the room.

"D.C. Greenshields you're on"

I got to my feet and followed him into the courtroom; the witness box was on my left just inside the door.

The judge was seated on a raised dais further to my left, the Fiscal and the defence team were seated around a large table in the middle of the floor, the jury were arranged behind them on a stepped gallery which was to enable every member of the jury a clear view of the witness giving evidence.

The accused was seated to my right between two uniformed police officers.

The public galleries were located further to my right, about twenty feet from the accused.

J.F. didn't even look at me when I entered the room, as I mounted the steps to the witness box I took a quick look at the people packing the public galleries.

They were packed in like sardines in a tin.

There must have been a couple of hundred people there to witness this spectacle and not a friendly face amongst them.

I recognised men and women, a real criminal 'who's who' from all over the East End of Glasgow sitting there. Calton must have been a very quiet place that day. My old enemy Dick Barton was in the room too. It crossed my mind that if he didn't like the result at the end of the trial he may try to burn this courthouse down also. He had tried that trick before at the High Court in Saltmarket when a result went against him.

They were all glowering at me, no Christmas cards again this year. I smiled over to them, took the oath and was led through my evidence by the Procurator Fiscal Depute.

There was actually very little in my evidence that was in any way contentious. I had simply been directed to the incident in response to a 999 call and on my arrival at the scene of the crime did all of the right things.

I had recovered the fence post which was later proved to be a weapon used in the assault, traced a witness to the deed and on receiving the crucial bit of information from the victim himself as to the identity of the assailant, I had gone through the correct procedures to obtain the warrant for his arrest.

Some members of the jury were passing notes amongst themselves, they'd noticed how many of the faces on the public benches were glaring at me, the hatred on their faces was plain to see.

The defence team would have been unaware of the jurors actions because they had their backs to the members of the jury.

The defence agent rose to his feet and gave me a long hard stare, to be honest, I think he was struggling to find anything very much to ask me.

I hadn't even alleged that his client had made a damning statement which would tend to show his guilt, (lawyers call such statements 'verbals').

I'd played it by the book and he was going to lose.

I fully expected at least one *'low bowler'* from this defence lawyer but it never came. This was the easiest ride I'd ever had in court and was really quite enjoying myself now.

After about forty minutes in the box I was excused and as I turned to exit from the witness stand I caught a glimpse of J.F looking at me, there was pure hatred in his eyes. The feeling was mutual. His entire family are evil and putting even just one of them to the sword was hugely satisfying.

Looking over to the public benches, I could see the same hatred in their faces too. There was a sensation of deep satisfaction coursing through my body, it is so good to know the low-lifes hate you; you are actually getting to them.

My partner Joe.C. was called into to court to give his evidence and was out less than twenty minutes later. He certainly did not get a hard time from the defence either. We hadn't given them anything to get their teeth into. It was straight down the middle.

I didn't hang about outside the court as the jury would still have to hear the closing speeches from the Crown and the Defence agent.

I doubted very much if J.F. would take the stand himself. The Crown prosecutor may have had a field day at his expense.

As we say in Glasgow: *"Your tea's out wee man."*

It was well and truly out of my hands now, the jury would decide J.F's. fate.

It's a bit of an anti-climax when you walk out of the court and the pressure is off.

Not that there was a lot of pressure on me on this occasion but you do tend to become quite uptight then suddenly it is all over. It's a bit like having s**.

No I won't go there.

I'd decided to call it a day, the motivation had gone for the moment, I would give myself a half day off, take a flier and be ready for the fray again tomorrow.

What would the jury's decision be? would he slip the net?

Early next morning just before 8a.m, the D/I came into the general office and made a bee-line for my desk.

'Did you get a result at the court yesterday?'

I had to tell him the jury was still out and I hadn't heard of any verdict as yet. I didn't want to tell him I'd given myself a *'flier'* and simply taken the rest of the afternoon off.

He told me to phone the effing Fiscal's Office and find out what the jury's verdict had been because the boss was asking.

I phoned my friend John D, the perennial Celtic fan at the Procurator Fiscal's office in Ballater Street and asked him to find out what the result had been and not to wind me up this time.

John was back on the phone within ten minutes, *'You've got a result there Wullie, Guilty and sentenced to 26 months in the jail'.*

I sought out the grumpy old D/I and gave him the good news.

He lifted his phone and called the Detective Superintendent who would then relay the information to the Divisional Commander.

The old sod then put the phone down and said: *"what time did you get home yesterday?"*

My hesitation gave the game away. He suspected me of taking the *'flier'*

"Ah thought so, you'll no be claiming that overtime then Wullie!"

The Cannabis Shop

Just along Bain Street near to Moncur Street, adjacent to the flat occupied by my earlier victim Robin there was a very curious shop indeed.

It was located on the first floor of a quite ornately built four storey red brick building which had arched windows and doorways. If my memory serves me correctly, the building originally housed a printing works but was later converted into an indoor market and various small shops.

This shop was located one up right as viewed from the street.

When I say this was a strange shop it is because it quite legally sold the various paraphernalia needed to smoke cannabis.

Buying or selling cannabis in resin, oil or herbal form is illegal, but selling the means to smoke them is not.

I had been told about the shop soon after it opened for business and just to satisfy my curiosity called in for a look at the merchandise on sale.

There were figures of the Buddha in different sizes from about six inches to approximately two feet in height.

Pipes with long stems, ornaments of eastern appearance, oriental rugs, multi-coloured hats with tassels and of course a multitude of hookahs which ranged from the basic water bottle with a long piece of tubing sticking out of it to the most ornately crafted pieces.

(A Hookah is an Eastern smoking pipe designed with a long tube passing through an urn of water which cools the cannabis smoke as it is drawn through, it is also known as a Hubble Bubble or a Bong).

The two people who ran the enterprise were a very pleasant young married couple; the male was aged about mid twenties, 5 feet 8 inches in height, slim build and had long hair with the obligatory pony tail.

His wife was probably about the same age, slightly smaller than he with collar length fair hair and to be honest was bordering on being a quite beautiful young woman.

I didn't and still don't agree with their line of business but it wasn't unlawful so really, it was of no concern to me how they made their living.

I'd done my *'nosey'*, looked around the shop then left to annoy some-one else. This was the Barras after all and I could always find some poor bugger to harass.

A few days later the almost inevitable occurred, the shop, which had only been open for about two weeks, was broken into over-night and practically all of the stock had been taken.

It fell to me to take on the enquiry,

I wasn't very busy at the time and was quite happy to make some enquiry into the incident.

The first thing to do of course was to visit the scene of the crime. I phoned the shop owner who lived in my home town of East Kilbride to arrange to meet him at his premises and made my way to his shop in Bain Street.

He was standing on the footway outside when I arrived and he immediately recognised me. Could have been my rather striking good looks he recalled or perhaps I was still wearing the same suit as before, probably the latter.

We climbed the well worn stairs to his shop, each step actually dipped in the centre from years of use, he unlocked the door to his premises and we entered. I have to admit to feeling sorry for the poor guy, what had been a well stocked room had been all but emptied of its contents. His business would very likely now go bust as he wasn't in a position to replace what had been stolen and there was no insurance cover. There was no chance of any reputable company taking on the risk of insuring a shop in this dilapidated building. Even the Mafia couldn't offer protection here. This was the Calton after all.

I was shown the point of entry, a window at the rear of the building measuring about 2 feet by 2 feet. The metal bars, not unlike those on a prison cell, which were intended to secure the window had been forced apart, the single glass window pane broken and entry gained.

The intruder or intruders had climbed onto the roof of a one storey building at the rear of his premises and forced entry from there.

I'd seen this modus operandi before. A scissors type car-jack is placed between the metal spars and cranked up using a lever. The spars are forced apart and being made of iron which is a soft metal, will bend quite easily.

I had a look around the place in the vain hope of finding a clue, more in hope than anything else; thieves don't often leave a driving licence, buroo card or business card with contact details on it.

My immediate thought was to suspect my *'friend'* Robin who lived next door to the place which had been broken into, but with nothing to go on at present he would laugh in my face and that would make me very, very unhappy.

The Scenes of Crimes Department at Police H.Q. were informed of the incident and with any luck they would find the clue which I couldn't, a fingerprint on the broken glass or something like that.

I would revert to type, this crime was without doubt the work of a native, about 99% of the crimes committed in or about the Calton were the work of the criminal element that lived there. I would have to make enquiries locally and I knew exactly who to start with.

It was often said that I'd friends in low places, the assertion was absolutely correct! Some of the people who spoke to me were a bit less than upstanding pillars of society.

I was a detective and thought like one, why ask a non-criminal who had committed a specific crime? Ask a criminal who was responsible for that crime because he or she would be more likely to know the answer to the question.

Calton was a tight community, the police were the enemy for many of the inhabitants and cultivating informants there was never easy but I had one and he was a Caltonian born and bred. A very rare occurrence indeed.

This man and I had crossed swords a few times and he had always lost the argument, much to his cost. I'd been responsible for having him banned from driving for 10 years and suffering a fine of £2,000. He didn't want to fall foul again.

We now had an understanding. He helped me with information and I stayed off his back. Simple! The system did work if handled properly.

All I had to do was phone his business telephone number, I was never under any circumstances to ring him at home or even speak to him in the street.

Any dealings between us were strictly in confidence.

If word escaped that he was a *'grass'* and to make matters worse he was actually *'grassing'* to me then his trading at the Glasgow Car Market would have to cease and his health would be at risk. Living or working in the Calton was not going to be an option.

I called him the following day and asked if he knew who had been responsible for the theft by housebreaking at the *'Cannabis Shop'* or if he didn't could he find out for me?

"Ah'll phone you the morra" was his response. I was quite confident that he would be as good as his word. He knows what I'm like when I'm upset and he had a business to run. Life could be made very difficult indeed for him. My nickname is so appropriate and wasn't earned easily.

I left it with him and went home, enough for one day!

The following morning I was back at my desk, the old D.I. came into the general office with the usual scowl across his ugly face.

He was a grumpy old sod but for all that I quite liked him, his heart was in the right place, he knew how to catch a thief and appreciated how I went about my business.

The boss would no doubt be putting pressure on the D.I. for results and the D.I. would in turn put the pressure on us *'pond life'* to get those results.

Shooting a glance in my direction he asked if I'd got a *'body'* lined up for the *'Cannabis Shop'* yet.

I'll never learn.

I replied: *"There are no definite lines of enquiry as yet sir but rest assured I'll leave no stone unturned in this investigation"*.

As he turned to walk away I heard him mutter: *"Cheeky bastard"*.

The day wore on and there had been no word from my Caltonian tout, the shop owner had compiled a list of the property which had been stolen from his shop, it ran into thousands of pounds in value.

He had even brought in some catalogues to show me the type of things which were missing.

I think I may just have known a Buddha figurine or a Hookah if I bumped into one of them in the dark.

When the D/I saw the value of the stolen property he would be more than ever concerned to have this one cleared up.

The fingerprint examination had been negative, nothing found at the point of entry and any impressions found in the shop would have been worthless as members of the public had access to the whole place.

I didn't really want to phone the informant again but time was wearing on, the more time passed by the more chance there was of the property being disposed of and the less chance of me recovering any of it.

About 2 o'clock in the afternoon I received a call on the police radio, I was to return to the police office immediately.

Had the old git seen the list handed in by the shop owner?

No he hadn't, the C.I.D. Clerk, the redoubtable Mr Harvey, had taken a phone call from a man who refused to give his name but had said: *"tell Greenshields the gear is in Balloch's hoose, he'll know whit ah mean"* and hung up the phone.

I knew exactly what and who he meant.

I went as a matter of urgency to the Glasgow District Court at 21 St Andrews Street where I sought out a Justice of the Peace who issued me with a warrant to search for specific items.

The warrant would also give me the power to force entry if required.

D.S. F. McC, a uniformed cop whose name escapes me at present and myself made our way to the house occupied by Balloch which funnily enough wasn't a million miles away from the shop.

Balloch was well known to me and I wasn't on his Christmas card list.

He could best be described as being a moron.

His flat was located above a row of shops in Abercromby Street across the road from the Bridgeton Health Centre. The only door to the dwelling was at the rear of the building and it was accessed from a gallery which spanned the length of the block.

It was highly unlikely that he would open the door to us.

I stood at the entrance to the health centre and looked up at his front window, there was movement apparent within the flat, that would do for me, no matter what happened now, his door was going to be opened.

The uniformed cop stood at the front of the building whilst the D/S and I went to the rear armed with a sledgehammer, I knocked on the door to the flat hoping he would simply come to the door and open it, fat chance!

He did come to the door but instead of opening up; he went away again and peered through a small window to the left of the door.

On seeing who was there, he ran back to the livingroom and opened his front window.

The cop we had left at the front came running and shouted to us that the clown was throwing articles out of the window into the street below.

No choice now but to smash down the door, the job did have some perks.

It only took a couple of hefty blows with the hammer and we were in. With the benefit of hindsight, I should perhaps have smashed his door down first and not bothered to knock. More of the stolen property could have been recovered intact if I'd given it a bit more thought.

He'd thrown a lot of property out of the window but there was still a large amount in his livingroom and bedroom.

The street outside was littered with debris, Buddha's, expensive Hookahs and loads of ornaments lay shattered on the roadway.

I fully expected him to put up a fight but sadly he just sat down on a couch without uttering a word and raised his hands as if to say *'handcuff me'*.

He wasn't to be disappointed.

Looking from his front window I was quite surprised to see his birdcage lying crushed on Abercromby Street, he had even thrown his pet budgerigar from the window and the cage had been run over by a passing car.

As I said, moron.

It was just a matter now of interviewing him and trying to elicit from him the names of his accomplices, he couldn't have done *'the turn'* on his own. There was never going to be the remotest chance of him telling us who was with him. I really wanted him to say Robin was there but that didn't happen.

Balloch was later charged with theft by housebreaking and I threw in the charge of murdering his budgie.

The inspector at the charge bar wasn't amused and gave me a stern look.

I had the remaining undamaged stock photographed before returning it to the owner who it has to be said was most grateful in the form of a large green coloured bottle containing a clear liquid.

His business continued there for a few more years but the local neds finally drove him away, the thieving from his shop was constant and the cost of replacing the lost stock was unsustainable.

Balloch went on to murder his girlfriend in a tower block in Dalmarnock by stabbing her multiple times about her head and body, I recall thinking at the time, *'that's the second burd he's killed'*.

Years later when I was working with the Drugs Squad at police H.Q. in Pitt Street, Glasgow I received information that a man who lived in East Kilbride was selling the controlled drug Cannabis resin from his home which was in the East Mains area of the town. The man's name meant nothing to me and didn't ring any bells.

Knowing my informant was usually correct as he smoked the dope himself and obviously knew where he could buy it, I did the usual things like having a look for myself and working out how best to approach the house without being seen. It would be fairly easy as the house was set in a cul-de-sac and could be approached along a lane which was accessed from another street not able to be viewed from the house to be searched.

We chose a Friday evening to do *'the turn'*. Six of us, two D.S.'s and four D.C.'s crept along the lane and into the wee porch at the front of the house.

The door was solid wood with no glass panels for the occupants to spy us through.

One of the D.S.'s knocked on the door, rank has its privileges and he was qualified to knock on doors.

It was opened a few seconds later.

I was standing at the back of the posse and couldn't see who opened the door but could hear a female voice

The door-knocking sergeant identified himself and told her the reason for our visit. The lady turned and walked back into the livingroom closely followed by ourselves, I was still at the rear and subsequently was last inside the house.

Sitting in an armchair was the owner of the *'Cannabis Shop'*, his wife who was standing by his side instantly recognised me too.

I was given a real telling off from the lady as she told me her husband liked to smoke a bit of dope and didn't harm anyone, he didn't even drink alcohol.

The husband looked at me and shook his head.

I don't make the rules, my job was to enforce them and selling Cannabis is still against the law. Whether you agree with it or not.

We were shown where his Cannabis was kept and didn't find any more than we were given by the occupants.

It did occur to me that there hadn't been any callers to the house in the time we were there. Maybe he was *'a dealer'*, maybe he wasn't.

If he was selling the stuff then it certainly wasn't on a grand scale.

He was reported to the Procurator Fiscal for possession of Cannabis Resin, a Class *'B'* controlled drug. A paper exercise only.

I don't know the outcome of the case but I would hazard a guess that at most he would have received a small fine or even just a warning letter. Certainly, to my knowledge anyway, it never saw the inside of a court-room.

As we live in the same town, I still see them about the place but with the passage of time they don't seem to recognise me now or maybe they just don't want to.

Can't really blame them.

Red sky at night

S tepping out from my front door late one summers evening to drive the relatively short distance to London Road police office to start my Sunday night shift, this would be my last night-shift for a month and I was looking forward to a couple to days off.

My attention was drawn to a glow in the Eastern sky over towards the city of Glasgow.

'Red sky at night, shepherds delight' an old saying meaning a good day would probably now follow.

Not in Glasgow, it meant something was burning.

Using my uncanny sense of direction, (my wife Margaret will fall about laughing when she reads this as she is well aware that I could get lost in my own home) I deduced that whatever was on fire would not be far from my patch in the East End.

It must have been quite some size of a blaze as I live about ten miles from the city and I could clearly see the glow illuminating the sky for miles around.

It's that sinking feeling again.

I kissed Margaret goodbye and whacked our two boys on the bottom just in case they misbehaved once I was safely out of sight.

The closer I got to Glasgow, the larger the glow in the sky became, there was little doubt in my mind it was at least going to be very close to the East.

Crossing Shawfield Bridge onto Bridgeton Main Street, the glow was now huge, it was in the direction of London Road police office and Celtic football ground.

I could now detect the smell of burning.

Driving along Dunn Street on the final leg of my journey to work, I saw that the blaze was in a small industrial estate in Fielden Street which separates the Barrowfield housing scheme from London Road police office.

A warehouse unit in the estate was well alight.

There must have been about half a dozen or more fire appliances at the scene and Fielden Street had been closed to all traffic.

Making my way into the C.I.D. general office, I found Det/Sergeant E. McC. there, he told me the premises occupied by a company who sold light fittings had gone up in flames about 9:00 p.m. and was a total loss. The remnants of the building would very likely have to be demolished as it was beyond saving.

There were no clues as yet as to the cause of the fire.

Any examination of the property would have to wait until daylight and of course the ashes would have to be allowed to cool.

I'd have to wait for my neighbour appearing and hope too that he would be sober, this particular partner had a habit of turning up for the night shift a bit the worse for wear.

For all that, he was a good guy with a heart of gold and would never do anyone a bad turn. He just had a wee problem.

There being nothing else on the go at the time, the late shift C.I.D cleared off a bit early, in police parlance they 'took a flier' after typing up their notes for the boss's information the next morning.

The report they left would include a reference to the fire in Fielden Street.

My neighbour did turn up and although there was a hint of beer from his breath, he was at least sober, for the present anyway.

He was as keen as me to get to the scene of the fire, even if we were just being a bit nosey.

Our uniformed colleagues let us through the cordon and onto Fielden Street, we parked our car about one hundred metres away from the smouldering ruin and made our way on foot to this scene of carnage. What had been a relatively new unit was now a shell. The flames had mostly been extinguished by the Fire Service and they were now spraying the remains of the warehouse unit with foam in an attempt to prevent the flames from flaring up again.

It was now safe enough for us to approach the building for a closer look.

I had some knowledge of the layout of the unit as I'd been the 'beatman' there for a time and had pulled the padlocks during my night-time patrols on many occasions.

Making my way to where the front door should have been, I found the steel roller-shutter door which secured the front entrance lying on the ground; it was still attached to some brickwork.

The bottom right corner of the steel door showed clear signs of having been tampered with, there was a cut of about nine inches in length in the metal. It seemed to be a freshly made incision as the steel showing at the cut was still bright.

I pointed it out to my colleague who was already making noises about visiting a local hostelry in Saltmarket not far from Glasgow Cross where we could have a beer before the publican went home.

Work first, then, if all was quiet much later on we could adjourn to the snooker room at one of the sub-offices for a frame or two and a can of beer.

A cut like that in a metal door could only have been made by someone using a power tool,

I wondered whether this could have been the cause of the fire. Had sparks or red-hot metal cuttings from the door ignited something inside the premises?

I called over the senior Fire Brigade officer and showed him what I'd found.

He had a look at the area immediately beside where the door had stood and agreed that it was highly probable the fire had started there.

In his opinion, he was the expert not me, this could well have been the seat of the fire.

This was now to be treated as a crime scene.

I arranged for a full Scenes of Crime examination to be carried out the next day, the Fire Service would also require to do their own examination of the site.

I took the precaution of having the metal door photographed in situ then taken to London Road police office for safe keeping; I had the feeling that it would be required later.

My suspicions were already turning towards the Barrowfield team.

This was their territory; the industrial estate sat right on the edge of the housing scheme, and was literally minutes walk from the safety of that warren of a place.

Where would a Barrowfield ned obtain a power saw? He would steal it of course.

We returned to the police office where I made a search of the records of thefts in the area going back for one month in time.

Sitting with a cup brown liquid, an imitation of coffee, I pored over green coloured paper files containing reports of theft, theft by opening lock-fast places, theft from motor vehicles and theft by housebreaking.

About an hour later I had one possible candidate, a Stihl saw had been stolen from the rear of a Glasgow City Council van which had been parked at the bottom end of *'wee Dalserf Street'* about a week before.

The saw had been used by workmen who were cutting concrete slabs on the footway there but when they returned to the vehicle after a tea break they discovered it had been broken into and a number of tools including the power saw and its accompanying petrol can had been removed.

There was every possibility that this was what I was looking for.

There were no suspects at the time for that crime and as it was of such a low priority in the great scheme of things I doubt very much if any thought was given to finding the culprit or culprits. It would simply have been written off as *'no witnesses, no suspects'* and consigned to history.

As time was now wearing on, it was well past the witching hour when all good Barrowfielders were in bed, I wouldn't be touring the streets looking for my next victim.

It occurred to me that there was one thing still to do before giving in to my neighbour and let him have a beer. The Stihl saw required petrol to drive its motor, perhaps, just perhaps, the thief or thieves would've had to buy fuel for the machine.

The closest petrol filling station to Barrowfield was located on Millerston Street near to Duke Street and as it was a twenty four hour garage the assistants may recall a sale of petrol to someone carrying a can.

If you don't ask, you don't get.

I dragged my thirsty partner along to the garage and asked the question.

The only assistant in the petrol station replied in the affirmative, yes, two scruffy young males had been there earlier and had bought a gallon of petrol which they had filled into a rather battered looking petrol can.

She remembered them in particular because they were four pence short of the cash required to pay for the fuel.

She had let them off with it and put the money in herself from some coppers which were kept in a saucer on the counter for just such an event.

The young lady thought they had been in the premises about seven o'clock on Sunday evening.

She didn't know their names but said she'd often seen them walking along the footway outside either coming from or going towards Barrowfield.

She would definitely be able to identify both males if she saw them again.

I noted a brief statement from the girl and obtained as good a description as was possible of the two men involved, this felt good, it just seemed as though I was on the right track.

The rest of that shift passed without further incident and we did get to play snooker and have a beer or two in 'the hut' behind Baillieston office along with our counterparts from Shettleston.

I left a big note for the information of the duty D/inspector detailing the events of the previous night and what the state of the game was now.

All that really had to be done was to show photographic images of the Barrowfield team to the shop assistant while the incident was still fresh in her mind. I then went home to enjoy my two days of rest before returning to the fray the following Wednesday.

Again, same routine, kiss Margaret and smack the children before leaving for work just to be sure they behaved whilst I was out.

I was a bit perturbed to discover that the incident at the lighting company had been allocated back to me for further enquiry.

Normally such an event would have been investigated by a senior officer; a building had been burnt down after all.

Still, no point in complaining. I was the pond life in this big pool and would just have to get on with it.

I obtained two sets of photographs and made my way along to the petrol filling station on Millerston Street. The young lady assistant looked through the collection presented to her and picked out two of the usual suspects.

Eddie McK. and Rab T.

This pair weren't only known to be associates of each other which tended to substantiate the identification, they were in fact full cousins and lived within five minutes walk of the now burnt out building.

All I had was them buying petrol before the building was destroyed, I'd need an awful lot more than that to put them before a court.

It's all very well knowing or strongly suspecting who had committed a crime, it has to be provable in a court of law. Without being a bit naughty!

The forensics tests at the scene wouldn't shed any light on the identity of those responsible. I'd have to try something else.

I believed I had enough circumstantial evidence to detain them both for interview but there is only one bite at the cherry. They couldn't be detained again on the same grounds if I failed to get the desired result at the first time of asking.

There would be a maximum of six hours of detention then it is a case of either charge or release them.

Rab T. would without doubt be the harder nut to crack, he simply would not admit to anything. I'd locked him up on numerous occasions and he would fight the case all the way. Every time he had been charged, he went to trial. There never was a plea of guilty from him.

I'd have to take my chances with Eddie; he was the softer option every time and besides he'd sell his granny down the river to save his own skin.

I let the following day, Thursday, come and go and went for my suspect Eddie early on Friday morning.

The one thing you had to remember when going to Eddie's house was to cover all of the exits.

He lived in a first floor flat in Fraser Street in the Barrowfield.

There were three bedroom windows to the front of the flat, a veranda at the side of the building and the livingroom, bathroom and kitchen windows at the rear.

When the police called there for any of the family, whether it was one of the five brothers who still lived there or perhaps one of the three ugly sisters an escape attempt would be made out of a window or the veranda door.

I went there well prepared, I was accompanied by the two 'beatmen'; two Barrowfield Liaison cops, members of a plain clothes team and of course my own neighbour.

There were two pairs of denim jeans hanging from a bedroom window, not because they had been washed and were hanging out to dry, they were just being aired before being worn yet again. This family were strangers to soap and water.

Four of us called at the door of the flat and after the usual pleasantries had been exchanged, Mary McK.. the matriarch of the clan admitted us to the hovel which was always warm and smelled of dirty feet.

I loved her one-liners, *"which ane ae ma boys will no be here for Christmas dinner this year Mr Greenshields?"*

"It's Eddie's turn Mary."

I think she actually loved me but was just too shy to say or perhaps this fat hag with her stockings rolled down to her knees, dirty grey hair and clothes that hadn't ever been washed was playing hard to get.

I would have given her a wee kiss if she'd asked, but no tongues OK?

We found Eddie concealed in a new hiding place, a cavity had been gouged out of a livingroom wall, just big enough to take one person in a crouching position.

The couch was then pushed up against the wall giving the appearance of there being no space behind it for a person to hide. Quite ingenious.

Eddie knew what to expect, if I came calling on a Friday morning he would be *'rattling'* by Friday afternoon and I had six hours to play with.

I think I omitted to fully explain to him why he was being detained but anyway, he didn't ask.

As we were leading him downstairs from the flat towards the close below a door was heard to slam shut after someone had called me a very dirty name.

Yet another year without a birthday or Christmas card from the delightful Mary. I'd forgotten to ask Mary for the loan of one of her used stockings to pop under my pillow at night. It would have cleared up my wee sinus problem in no time!

I put Eddie in a detention room after the preliminaries had been completed and went for what could very loosely be described as a coffee from the dispensing machine in the canteen. 10p for a number 37. White coffee with no sugar and probably no coffee either. This was possibly the same stuff the Germans drank in place of coffee during the last bit of unpleasantness, made from roast and powdered acorns.

It was almost eight o'clock and the Herald crossword was still untouched.

He'd now been told he was being detained because of the fire, I didn't need to say which fire I was referring to, he knew without me having to explain any further.

Two hours passed by and Eddie hadn't yet cracked, I'd give him another hour at most, then no more Mr Nice Guy. The thumbscrews would be produced.

I needn't have worried my pretty head; the door to the C.I.D. office opened and in came the turnkey, the man who was responsible for looking after the prisoners and detainees.

He made a beeline towards my desk and said something very uncomplimentary about my parentage. This man did not believe I knew my father.

If there were no people in the cells or detention rooms then he could have an easy shift, I was the cause of him actually having to get off his backside and do what he was being paid for.

The lazy sod informed me that a prisoner in one of the detention rooms wished to speak to me.

The *Glasgow Herald* crossword had been completed so I was now free to deal with Eddie.

I summoned my neighbour from the rest room and we both hustled the poor man along to the interview suite, the rubber room, where the truth could be extracted from him. I'd missed my calling. A wee job with the Spanish Inquisition would've done nicely. Torquemada eat your heart out.

Eddie would without doubt stay true to form; he always started off by lying through his teeth then gradually bit by bit the story would change as his teeth became fewer until eventually what had really occurred emerged from his bleeding mouth.

The interview rooms were bare except for four metal chairs and a table, a tape recording device sat on the table.

I never allowed as much as an ash-tray in the interview room, anything like that was a potential weapon for a prisoner to use and quite naturally some prisoners got angry during questioning.

I began by asking Eddie who had broken into the Glasgow City Council works van in *'wee Dalserf Street'*, if he hadn't done it himself he'd soon tell me who did.

Eddie had no qualms regarding talking to the police when he may have something to gain from it.

"Am ah getting oot the day Mr Greenshields?" asked Eddie. He was always respectful and knew how to address higher life forms than himself.

His possible release would depend on how much he helped me was the response.

The ground rules had now been established.

"Rab T... done it."

That made sense; Rab lived in a first floor flat at the bottom end of *'wee Dalserf Street'* along with his ugly witch of a girlfriend Geraldine McG.

I believe both should've been neutered as the thought of them breeding and spawning yet more Rabs and Geraldines is almost unbearable.

The van had been broken into right outside Rab's close, he only had to emerge from his lair, break into the van and disappear back into the close again with his loot.

Eddie went on to tell me he had seen the Stihl saw the previous day, it was lying on Rab's livingroom floor.

I still had a bit of time to play with as Eddie's detention was still lawful for three hours or so.

Now for the hard question.

"Did you burn the factory down on purpose or was it an accident Eddie?"

I referred to the premises as a factory because Eddie wouldn't know what a warehouse was.

His mouth fell open; this was a real low-bowler, quite unexpected.

He obviously knew I'd ask him about the fire but I went straight for the jugular instead.

I told him that no matter what happened he would be charged with attempting to break into the warehouse with intent to steal and maybe even with intentionally burning the place down with the resultant damage being estimated at over one million pounds.

The figure of one million pounds meant nothing to him, his brain had no conception of anything over a tenner.

Eddie sat very quietly for a couple of minutes gathering his thoughts and staring at the floor.

"Ah never done it Mr Greenshields, it wis Rab T..., we were gonnie tan the light factory an he hud the big saw hing, Rab wis cutting the door when we saw smoke coming fae inside the place. We jist f****d off cos it wis on fire."

Eddie was told he was now under arrest, I charged him with attempting to break into the warehouse and reckless conduct with regards to the fire. The Fiscal could change the charges if he wished.

Eddie would be detained in custody prior to appearing at Glasgow Sheriff Court on Monday.

I had the identification from the petrol station employee and Eddies own admission as to his involvement; that would suffice for the moment.

We took him back to the detention area and informed the duty inspector of the developments, he agreed, Eddie was staying until Monday.

The lazy turnkey was hovering about in the background glowering at me, I smiled back at him, well what passes for a smile, smiling was never a strongpoint of mine.

I very quickly typed up a request for a Justice of the Peace search warrant, if Rab had the Stihl saw in his flat I was entitled to search for that piece of equipment.

I phoned a J.P. who lived in nearby Comelypark Street and explained the circumstances to him; I asked if he was available to sign the warrant. No problem, he would do that.

Collecting my team of *'Untouchables'* we made straight for the J.P.'s home which was in nearby Slatefield Street where the necessary paperwork was completed and from there we made the very short journey across the Gallowgate and into the land that time forgot, Barrowfield.

Two cops at the front and another two at the rear of the block of flats which was the second last close in *'wee Dalserf Street'* at its junction with Stamford Street. Directly across the road from *'the Welma'* bakery.

Myself and three others climbed the stairs, the close smelled like a public toilet, it stank of stale urine and had probably never been washed, not with water anyway.

Rab's door had four locks on it, perhaps there were thieves about and he was being security minded.

We knocked on the door although neither Rab nor Geraldine would have any intention of opening it.

If the saw was still there, he couldn't get rid of it now and throwing it from a window wasn't going to solve his problem. We were there and we were going to enter the flat no matter what.

As it wasn't yet midday Rab would probably still be in bed with Geraldine, how repulsive, the very thought of it makes me shudder.

I knocked on the door again and could hear the sound of shuffling feet and muffled voices within but still no-one came to answer it.

Plan 'B'

Fetch the sledgehammer from the car and if the door remained closed our *'large key'* would soon open it.

Rab and Geraldine still ignored our requests to open up; did they really think we would give up and go away? Not a hope in hell.

One of the plainers took charge of the *'door opener'* and with two blows had removed the door from its hinges.

Neds simply don't learn, it doesn't matter how many locks they put on a door, it still only has two or at best three hinges and that is the side to strike with a large hammer. It very rarely failed.

Scrambling over the matchwood that used to be his door we entered the livingroom where Rab and Geraldine were sitting on a couch, both with quite startled expressions on their faces, perhaps they hadn't heard us knocking on the door or even smashing it down.

A very bad case of East End deafness.

I showed them the warrant and asked if there was by chance a large petrol driven saw to be found in the flat.

Rab wasn't pleased and grunted back: *"Don't hink so."*

English translation; *"Not to my knowledge"*.

I think he may just have noticed a rather large, smelly power saw in his home but then again the stink of he and Geraldine in the place may just have been sufficient to mask the odour of a petrol engine.

An old petrol driven saw would've smelled sweeter than this pair of cretins.

There was a suspicious looking bump in a coat which was lying behind their couch. How cunning can these devils be?

I lifted the coat and there it was, a big yellow coloured power saw.

"Oh look Rab, how did that get there, did Santa come early? Get your jacket on".

A battered and well used old petrol can containing some liquid was also found in a wardrobe in the bedroom.

As usual, Rab was saying nothing.

Interviewing this one would be easy, apart from giving us his name and confirming his date of birth he would remain totally silent.

A real *'no comment'* interview.

He was also detained for an appearance at Glasgow Sheriff Court the following Monday.

I could now put pen to paper and prepare a fairly tight case against both.

I had the remains of the metal door and the cutting wheel from the Stihl saw taken to the Forensic Laboratory at police headquarters in Pitt Street, Glasgow and requested that an examination be made to establish whether the cut in the door could have been caused by the blade from that saw.

To my untrained eye it appeared that the blade fitted the damaged door perfectly but I'd have to let the experts at the lab give me their opinion in the form of a *'lab report'* which I'd then take to the Fiscal's Office for his information.

Much to my delight, they were both remanded in custody to await trial, which under Scots Law would require to be held within 110 days.

I'd have my forensic report long before the trial date.

About a month later I was in possession of a document which told me the incision in the metal door had in fact been caused by the blade of the Stihl saw and that fragments of metal found on the blade had probably come from the door.

Game, set and match.

The trial date came around and not unusually, Eddie changed his plea to one of Guilty. Rab was advised by his lawyer that under the circumstances it wasn't advisable for him to adhere to his *'not guilty'* plea as Eddie could now be used as a witness by the Crown. Eddie would sell his cousin down the river if put in the witness box.

I sat in the court as both were sentenced to the maximum term of two years in prison.

'Smug' doesn't even begin to describe my feelings at that time.

Rab had committed a theft by housebreaking in East Kilbride a few years earlier which my wife Margaret and I had actually witnessed and reported to the local police office and to two C.I.D officers at the London Road office as the Barrowfield housebreaking team would be making their way back to the East End where they lived.

All three officers through a mix of laziness and incompetence did absolutely nothing and Rab escaped with a lot of jewellery *(pages 17 and 18 of Greenshields - A Glasgow Cop)*

He was now getting his just reward. What goes around comes around.

Eddie's mother, Mary, was right again. One less for Christmas dinner.

I had mixed feelings about Eddie going to jail, solving crimes in the East End would be that bit harder now as he was a great source of information for me.

He was a grass, an informant, a tout. His information went a long way to paying off my mortgage and giving my wife and family some great holidays.

Thanks Eddie!!

The warehouse was never rebuilt, the business moved to a safer location somewhere in the south of the city.

The Inspector

Some people are stupid and others are incompetent, I actually came across one person in the police service who suffered from both of these defects.

Bearing in mind the fact that I don't tell lies now I'm retired from the job, this true story has to be told. It shows how even a moderately high ranking officer can commit the most unbelievably naive acts of pure folly.

My turn at night shift had come around again all too quickly, Det/Sergeant Felty had taken some leave and as it was never really advisable to work a late shift or night shift alone in the East I was partnered by a cop from one of the uniform shifts until my own *'neighbour'* returned from his break.

I'd worked with this man for a short time whilst I was still a uniformed constable and held him in high esteem; he was a real worker who got results and wasn't afraid to lead from the front.

I'll refer to him as Des; he's still a serving officer so I'll not give any clues as to his real identity.

Des will no doubt recognise himself and the facts of this sorry tale.

Our shift began at 11p.m. on a Monday night, I tidied up some of the paperwork which had accumulated whilst I was on dayshift.

Night shift could be quite handy for putting pen to paper, writing police reports and generally clearing my feet of the accumulated bumph before starting all over again when that shift had finished and I was again working in daylight.

Des asked if I was *'up'* for doing a wee drugs turn with him later that night if all remained quiet, he'd received reliable information to the effect that a man who lived in the multi-storey block at number 112 Baltic Street in Dalmarnock had possession of about five kilos of the controlled drug Cannabis Resin in his flat which was located on an upper floor of the building.

I was aware that Des could almost hear the grass growing in that part of town, his information was usually correct so I would go along with the plan.

About midnight, I asked Des to call in at the uniform bar area to check for any crime reports which may have come in and we'd not been informed of.

Some cops actually took reports of incidents which would require C.I.D attention and simply failed to tell us about the matter.

It was good practice to check the C.I.D. *'dookit'* at the front office frequently.

Des almost took the door to the C.I.D. room off its hinges as he came scurrying back in.

The man he'd told me about earlier was being held in the cells, he'd been arrested by a couple of the uniform beatmen for committing a Breach of the Peace on Dalmarnock Road just as the pubs were closing and had been brought into London Road office.

This was going to be like taking sweeties from a wean.

We made our way through the office to the charge bar where we found the duty officer, a female Inspector with a face like a horse but less intelligent.

Des and I informed her of the circumstances surrounding the prisoner having a quantity of Cannabis Resin in his flat and requested that he be held until we'd called at a local Justice of the Peace and obtained a warrant to search the flat for controlled drugs.

She agreed to hold onto him meantime and we made our way back to the C.I.D. room from where I phoned the J.P. She agreed to sign the Pro Forma warrant which Des was busily typing out.

It only took Des about ten minutes to type out the document, I read it over to check for any errors and finding there were none we left for the Justice's home which was across the road from the Barras market in Bain Street.

The lady came to the door in her housecoat, I think we probably got her out of her bed, it was after midnight.

I explained the circumstances and handed the warrant request over to her, she read it through, put me on oath then signed the piece of paper.

Why can't it always be so easy?

Well it wasn't easy, on our return to the police office we found that the prisoner had been released by that horses arse of an Inspector.

I was stunned. She was seated at her desk in the bar area when I approached her.

I had to ask the very obvious question, why?

The Inspector replied that his home address had been verified and she no longer required to hold onto him. She'd told him that the C.I.D. would speak to him later regarding another matter.

She looked away, the conversation was over.

There was no debate, I was a detective constable and she was the Inspector.

Des and I hurried from the office and sped to the block of flats which is within spitting distance of the police station. It was now about 1a.m. and the city streets were deserted.

Walking towards the rear of the building where his flat was located we saw what we'd been half expecting.

Scattered all over the footway was the resin. It had been tossed out of a window, he knew we were going to call armed with the warrant to search his flat and had dumped the drugs.

We'd lost.

Stupidity and incompetence had cost us an easy capture.

I did leave a note for the Det/Inspector explaining what the fool had done but I also knew that no action would be taken. She was a rising star and I was a foot soldier.

Some months later I emerged from Glasgow Sheriff Court in Carlton Place.

I'd been called to give evidence at a trial there and had been released from the Court about mid-day.

The female Inspector was standing on the pedestrian concourse outside the court building in full uniform, holding hands with her husband in full view of the public and the neds who were milling around the place.

Less than professional. I wanted to cringe.

I've never seen her again but did hear she'd been promoted to Chief Inspector.

The mind boggles, as if it wasn't bad enough that she moved onward and upwards. Who in the corridors of power in police headquarters thought highly enough of this waste of space to recommend her for promotion in the first place? Sleep easily in your bed tonight, the community is safe in their hands.

On the tiles

This isn't a tale of the boys' night out unfortunately, it is a true tale regarding a company who were at the time located in Broad Street, Bridgeton.

This company supplied flat pack kitchens and tiles to all and sundry, whether it was members of the public, self employed kitchen fitters and tilers or even large retail outlets who bought the items at discounted prices and thereafter sold them on to the public at *'bargain prices'*.

Our C.I.D. clerk Ian Harvey was sitting at his desk early one Tuesday afternoon when he noticed a man standing at the public reception window, the man was smartly dressed in a dark coloured business suit and looked to be quite perplexed.

This customer was a bit out of the ordinary for Ian to deal with, he usually dealt with the residents of nearby hostels who were claiming to have lost their *'Giro's'* and would ask Ian for *'a pink slip'* which they could then produce at the local Benefits office in order to claim another payment.

Ian was very diplomatic with these claimants and his usual two word response ended with the word: *"off"*.

This fellow wasn't requesting a pink slip however.

He was in fact the General Manager of the tile supplying company and was normally based in Dartford in Kent in his native England, the Broad Street warehouse being a large subsidiary of the English side of the business.

This distraught little Englander said there were huge discrepancies in the stocks which had only been discovered after an unannounced visit to Broad Street by himself and the company auditors.

There were literally hundreds of thousands of tiles missing and hundreds of entire flat packed kitchens were also unaccounted for.

Ian, thinking on his feet as usual decided correctly to arrange for the General Manager to speak directly with the Det/Inspector who was on duty that day.

An allegation of theft or fraud of this magnitude should perhaps be dealt with by a senior supervisory officer. He would have to be made aware of the circumstances anyway.

(Personally, I quite liked the Det/Inspector but we haven't been exchanging Christmas cards recently). Must have been something I said!

The D/I was summoned from his lair and listened intently to what was being reported by the be-suited Kentishman.

He decided that on the face of it there may have been a crime committed here and it should be investigated by C.I.D. officers, not including him, but by the pond-life who existed on the other side of the corridor which separates the privileged classes from the serfs.

I cannot recall in detail who all were despatched the short distance to the warehouse, it's only about five minutes walking distance from the police office.

Det/Sergeant F. McC. was there as were Det/Constable J.C. and myself.

As I recall there were another three or four detectives in attendance too.

Our instructions from the Det/Inspector were quite explicit, we were to gather up every member of staff there, convey them to London Road police office and take full statements from everyone.

The interview rooms at the police station were full and every available space with the exception of the Det/Inspectors room was pressed into service.

I interviewed one person; he was actually the warehouse manager, in the identification parade waiting room which I'd commandeered for myself.

This man was the most unlikely *'manager'* I'd ever come across.

He was only about thirty years of age, timid in the extreme, tall and very fat, he lived with his mother in the family home on Shettleston Road which if you know the East End isn't really that far away from his place of employment.

He simply hadn't a clue about what if anything had been going on there under his nose. I still to this day don't believe he was in any way complicit in or aware of any wrongdoing.

He was in my own opinion just incompetent and had been promoted to a position beyond his capabilities.

A fault of his employers down south, not his.

The employees were all released after interview and allowed by the General Manager to return to work meantime.

I watched with much amusement in the *'corridor of power'* as the Det/ Sergeant handed a pile of handwritten interview statements to the Det/Inspector who promptly handed them back with the words *'It's your enquiry now Frank'*.

I don't think there was much love lost between them and if the senior of the two allocated an enquiry to the junior one then there could be no argument.

Unless of course the Sergeant passed the buck and allocated the work further down the chain of command.

I promptly made myself scarce.

It wasn't really the work entailed in the investigation that bothered me, it was the fact that two officers of higher rank had decided not to get involved because it might get quite complicated. Either that or they simply couldn't be bothered.

The gents toilet in the gymnasium would suffice, the Det/Sergeant would look for me in the snooker room or the canteen on the top floor, knowing me to be totally against any form of exertion (with a very few exceptions of course) he would never even consider that I should be in the gym. The very thought of me being found in a gym makes me shudder.

The only other time I was to be found in that place was when there had been an attempted murder in the Mecca Bar at Glasgow Cross and everyone in the bar at that time had been taken to London Road office and because there were so many of them they were housed in the gym before being interviewed.

I will never forget to my dying day looking in through the double doors from the corridor outside the Detective Sergeants room into the gymnasium and seeing about forty regulars from the Mecca holding an impromptu dance.

One wee woman who walked with the aid of a zimmer frame was waltzing with a male companion who was also holding onto the frame. He let go and collapsed onto the floor. He was so drunk, only her walking aid had been keeping him upright.

She was further contributing to the party atmosphere by leaving a trail of pee behind her as she now danced solo across the floor.

The customers of Leo Francetti, manager of the Mecca Bar had to be seen to be believed.

Anyway, I digress, my ploy was successful and my neighbour J.C. had been cornered in the snooker room by the devious detective sergeant who was simply passing the buck further down the chain. Instead of me poor J.C'd been lumbered with this potential horror bag.

Being a helpful soul, when told of this foul act I of course offered to assist him with the enquiry. The investigation was his responsibility and I would be the willing Captain Hastings to his Poirot.

I really do have a heart of gold or is that rightly a heart of shit?

The latter may be more accurate I think.

J.C. was a smashing guy but this enquiry terrified him, he'd never even been involved with anything remotely similar before and was struggling with it.

Give him any amount of run of the mill violence, dishonesty or drugs and he would take it in his stride, but this was a slightly different ball game.

A series of thefts going back possibly over a number of years which would probably have cost the company involved somewhere in the region of a million pounds or more and the supervisors on duty that day were avoiding it like the plague. I hope they read this and will no doubt recognise themselves. Shame on you!

J.C., the poor sod, was waffling and didn't know which direction to take so I suggested we find out from the General Manager what exactly the audit had revealed and what had been the results from any previous audits.

Had there been any major discrepancies before and what had been behind the unannounced swoop by auditors and the General Manager himself?

A meeting was later arranged whereby the Financial Director, Company Secretary and General Manager accompanied by the company solicitor of the tile supplier would attend at London Road office on a Thursday morning. J.C. and I would go over the results of the past three audits and financial returns of the Broad Street branch with them and try to work out where and when the problem arose.

Thursday was of course the last day of my early shift; I would have yet another week of night duty to endure shortly.

I turned up as usual for work a bit early, I was at my desk just before eight o'clock on the Thursday morning. Ian, the C.I.D. Clerk was sitting at his desk and smiling over in my direction. He was either going to give me another hard enquiry or he knew something I didn't yet know.

"Your neighbour phoned in sick", he said.

Why did that not surprise me? My heart sank into my boots.

The management team from the tile company were due to meet with us at ten o'clock and my neighbour had taken *'a sicky'*.

I approached the Det/Sergeant to ask for a bit of assistance and was told that I could have the use of his room when interviewing my visitors.

That wasn't the sort of help I was looking for.

He pulled on his coat and disappeared out of the office for the rest of the morning.

There was no alternative now but simply to get on with it.

The company directors turned up right on schedule at the C.I.D. reception window, Ian called me over, he was still grinning from ear to ear as he introduced me to the men in smart suits which put my Ralph Slater number to shame. I wasn't about to be cheeky to the C.I.D. Clerk, I'd long since learned my lesson in that department. When you're already in a hole, it isn't advisable to dig it any deeper. I knew to my bitter experience about the horror stories he kept in his bottom drawer beside his packets of McVities digestive biscuits.

I shook hands with the businessmen and showed them along the corridor past the Det/Inspector's room which for some strange reason had the door closed.

It wasn't normally shut when he was there.

I sat behind the sergeant's desk which made me feel very important, (my arse), the men in suits pulled up chairs and gathered round. Sheafs of paper were produced from their briefcases and laid on the desk.

The Financial Director did most of the talking and led me through the company's financial returns for the previous four years.

He showed me sets of figures that clearly showed how the Glasgow branch had plummeted from being a very profitable enterprise to now being such a liability that the very existence of the whole company was in doubt.

The latest stocktaking check showed that there was a black hole into which not far short of one million pounds worth of company stock, tiles and flat pack kitchens had disappeared.

There was no paperwork to show that it had been sold.

Here was I, a rookie detective constable being left to get on with the enquiry, but I'm not bitter. Am I?

The profits had declined sharply over a three year period, fours years' back it had been trading very profitably, three years back it was still in profit but less so than before, two years back it barely broke even and when the audit for the previous year was taken it was almost one million pounds in the red.

This clearly wasn't a bit of pilfering from the employer, there was another company being run within the legitimate one.

To my way of thinking, there was obviously more than one person involved in this scheme and the warehouse staff who actually despatched the goods were the main suspects. Anything leaving the premises would have to be handled by them.

The decline in profits had begun to show three years back, who had been recruited since the company was in profit and was still there at present?

Perhaps that was being a bit simplistic but to my way of thinking it was also logical.

Before the gentlemen took their leave I asked if I could be supplied with a complete list of employees for the previous six years. I wanted everything they had on the staff there, names, dates of birth, home addresses and previous employment history.

This request was not to be made known to anyone at the Broad Street warehouse, not even the management there.

I showed the by now quite satisfied Directors out from the police office and returned along the corridor past the now open Inspectors door to the sergeants room where I lifted a pile of papers from an in-tray and an out-tray, shuffled them like a pack of cards and placed them neatly back into the trays. The bastard could sort that lot out himself.

J.C. had 'diked' the enquiry onto me, he wasn't now going to get it back, I had my teeth into it, and this enquiry was now mine.

Turning up on the Monday night for the start on my night shift, I wasn't surprised to see J.C. there. His sudden illness had just as suddenly gone and he was well again.

He asked how the interview with the Company Directors had gone as soon as I entered the C.I.D general office, not *'did you have a good week-end?'* or *'How are you?'*

It must have preyed on his mind all week-end.

I wasn't for telling him too much and simply said: *"it was OK"*

The list of employees was in my dookit the following night.

I had a quick look through it and saw there was very little in the way of staff turnover. Only two men had joined the company in the relevant period and both worked in the despatch department. A big clue eh?

I made my way through the building and into the control-room where I asked one of the staff to run a criminal records check on both males.

Sometimes it's like spearing fish in a barrel.

Both were convicted thieves and were known to have been associates long before taking up employment with the now almost bankrupt company.

Neither were married and both lived in rented accommodation in adjacent multi-storey blocks in East Kilbride.

My intention was to detain them for interview when my next day-shift week came around. I still believed that others were involved but I suspected this pair to be the main players.

It's amazing how many people want in on the act when it's all coming together.

I'd been left alone to get on with the hard bit, now J.C. and a certain Det/Sergeant wanted in on the act.

J.C. would be coming to the warehouse with me anyway as he was my partner but I wouldn't be inviting the sergeant along.

The dayshift duly came around again, J.C. and I collected another two detectives and called at the warehouse in Broad Street fully expecting to find the *'bad men'* there.

What a let down, neither had been at work for about a week and there had been no contact with either of them.

As the management at the place had no knowledge of my understanding with the Directors down south, they wouldn't have known to contact me when this pair disappeared from the scene so quickly.

I feared the worst now, J.C. and I made our way to one tower block in East Kilbride whilst the other team went to another.

The flat I attended at was unoccupied when I got there and enquiries with neighbours revealed the occupant had left for America or Canada quite suddenly the previous week taking only a small suitcase with him.

The other team got the same response.

I checked with the airline companies flying to North America and found both men had booked seats on the same flight from Glasgow to New York a week before and both only had hand luggage.

They had milked their employer for God only knows how much money and now had slipped the net.

I hate losing and wasn't best pleased. Extradition proceedings would have to be considered now.

Having made contact with the Financial Director again, I informed him of the development and was a bit surprised to be told that he was satisfied with my efforts and that the culprits had been identified. I was asked to let the matter drop and not to pursue it further. His decision, not mine.

The company would survive and the General Manager whom I'd first spoken of would take control of the Broad Street warehouse with immediate effect.

There were now a couple of vacancies in the warehouse and not being slow I suggested to the director that I knew of an honest 18 year old boy who was leaving school that very week. He could do no better than have him interviewed for a post with his company.

The young man was duly seen and started work on the 'shop floor' the following week.

My nephew's still there and is now the manager.

Giant Haystacks

Away back in the mists of time when I was a young constable pounding my beat along Duke Street and the *'Drives'* area of Dennistoun I came across a mountain of a man who drove a black Hackney Taxi-cab. At first sight he appeared to be a monster.

Even when just sitting behind the wheel of his cab you could tell he was an enormous size of a man

Walking the beat in Dennistoun on night shift could be almost soul destroying at times,

My wife Margaret, bless her, claims that couldn't happen to me as I don't possess a soul anyway. Apparently Satan bought it from me years ago.

If there was nothing happening the hours would drag by and there were very few places open where a cup of tea or coffee could be begged.

One bolt-hole on my beat was the taxi office at the top of Millerston Street; it was open all night and only closed about seven o'clock in the morning which was when my shift ended too.

The taxi haven was where I first came across big Robert.

It was a miserably wet night and as usual there was nowhere to go, I was quite new to the area having only recently been moved there from the Dalmarnock and Bridgeton area. Like a fish out of water.

I was still finding my feet and trying to get to know the people who lived and worked in Dennistoun.

Taking the bull by the horns I decided to give it a try and entered the taxi drivers' rest room with rainwater running in streams down my raincoat and into my boots.

The place was warm and smoke filled, it smelled of fried sausages and bacon.

There were groups of men seated all around the place and one group of about eight or more were playing cards, *'Nominations'* I believe the game is called.

The buzz of conversation ceased as I entered the room, they all eyed me suspiciously, this was obviously not the norm, and maybe the beat-man didn't usually frequent this place. Had I made a mistake?

There was an awkward silence for a few seconds and then up from the card table rose this giant of a man who immediately reminded me of Giant Haystacks, a once famous 1960s and 70s Saturday afternoon T.V. all-in wrestler. He was easily six feet six inches in height with an enormous barrel chest and big bushy beard which almost hid his face. He had hands like shovels.

The colour must have drained from my normally ruddy cheeks as this beast looked me up and down; had I just entered the bear pit?

Instead of picking me up and breaking me into little pieces he said, *'like a cup of tea wee man?'* I mumbled my thanks and he paid the girl behind the counter the nominal fee of five pence before returning to his card game.

I stood near to the gas fire and warmed myself whilst watching with interest as bundles of banknotes changed hands during the game with steam rising from wet hat, coat, trousers and boots.

There was more money on that table than Margaret took for her housekeeping every month.

My presence was gradually being accepted by the drivers and the talking resumed although it was a bit more muted now, perhaps there were things being said that a *'copper'* shouldn't know about.

I had, though, broken the ice and if I did chance my arm again then the shock of seeing a uniformed cop in their territory might not be so great next time.

About ten minutes had passed and I decided it was time to leave, enough for one night.

Having dried myself, been warmed by the gas-fire and with a large mug of hot tea inside me I thanked Robert who was still throwing wads of money into the *'pot'* and left the taxi rest.

Robert looked up as I was nearing the door and said something about seeing me again.

I took that to mean I could come back.

As fate would have it the rest of the night shift week was quite busy with mostly minor domestic disputes and the like, nothing too serious but time consuming nevertheless. (Nowadays the husband is locked up if there is even a suspicion of domestic violence, back then they were both told to *'calm it'* and the male advised to go for a walk until the tempers had cooled.)

Still, when you are busy the time just flies in and the worst shift in the world is soon over.

I became a regular visitor to the taxi drivers bothy over the next few months and was now pretty much accepted by them and Robert was usually there or thereabouts to buy me a mug of tea. I was never allowed to put my hand in my pocket and was beginning to strike up a bit of a rapport with most of them. I never took part in the gambling though; I am not nor ever could be a gambler besides not being able to afford to sit at the table with men who gambled away literally hundreds of pounds at a sitting.

I would grudge losing a couple of pounds on a racehorse never mind hundreds of pounds on the turn of a card.

As I trudged my way about Dennistoun, taxi drivers would acknowledge me by sounding a toot on the horn as they passed by and give me a wave.

I was an accepted fixture on Duke Street now.

About 2 o'clock one morning I was walking along a deserted Duke Street towards Garfield Street when a black taxi cab pulled up beside me, the driver was none other than the big fellow, Robert.

"Wullie", he said, *"There's a guy running down Cumbernauld Road carrying a sewing machine"*. He pointed back towards the direction he'd just come from.

I thanked him and he drove off towards the City Centre.

I turned the volume control on my police radio down very low and stood just inside the mouth of a close in Duke Street near to Garfield Street with my uniform cap off and waited for a few minutes.

Sure enough, there he was, peering round the corner of Cumbernauld Road and Duke Street to see if there was anyone about before venturing further.

It was an old *'friend'* of mine Davie B, a junkie thief and housebreaker who lived in nearby Bellfield Street with his widowed mother. He'd obviously been out earning money for the next *'hit'*.

This was too easy, he was on his own and if he was making his way home all I had to do was stand in the close, wait until he drew level and ambush him.

He must have read the script, I waited for the right moment and he was drawn by the neck into the close.

Davie, seeing I was on my own opted to make a fight of it, a bad choice I don't use the Marquis of Queensberry rules and a boot in the testicles often offends.

Whilst he was on his knees being sick I handcuffed him and sent for the divisional van which was driven by my pal *'big Jock Gillespie'*.

Davie would be going to Glasgow Sheriff Court the following day.

The sewing machine had a serial number and the words *'Glasgow C.C. Education Dept'* painted on one side.

Pound to a penny the machine was the proceeds of theft by housebreaking at a school.

Having secured my prisoner at London Road police office, I attended at the nearby Whitehill Secondary School which is close by Cumbernauld Road.

There would no doubt be a broken window or a door lying open, Davie had no finesse, there was absolutely nothing subtle about him. He was just crude.

Sure enough, a window on the ground floor giving access to a Domestic Science lab had been smashed. (Is it still known as Domestic Science, I'm afraid I'm a bit of a dinosaur and still tend to use old terminology).

I wasn't about to climb in through the broken window; all I'd require to do was have the janitor summoned from his bed to allow me access to the classroom. There would probably be a space on a desk where a sewing machine should be sitting.

Too easy, I waited until the Janitor arrived, he let me into the school and the empty space was there for all to see. A row of machines with a gap in it.

Davie wasn't best pleased to see me again at the office and was still nursing his very tender bits; the moral of the story is don't offer to fight with the dirtiest fighter in school. I'm a Shettleston boy remember. My good looks were preserved by retaliating first.

Standing toe to toe with a ned whilst trading punches never appealed to me.

He was even less pleased when I charged him with theft by housebreaking at Whitehill Secondary School.

A quick custody case was rattled out and he was ready for another appearance at court courtesy of that bastard Greenshields and an anonymous passing taxi-driver.

More joy was yet to come, as Davie lived within the boundaries of my beat I would have the great pleasure in telling his mother who hated the sight of me that her son would not be home for breakfast that morning.

It's the little things in life that make it so pleasing.

The years rolled on and I *'progressed'* from being a uniformed pond life to becoming a be-suited grim faced detective. Robert and I kept up contact and would sometimes bump into each other as he plied his trade and I mine.

He disappeared from the scene and after not seeing or hearing anything with regard to his wellbeing or otherwise for quite some time I was surprised to hear one morning as I was taking up duty that he was in custody at London Road, charged with having committed a serious assault.

Robert had been working as the manager of the Overdale Bar which stood at the corner of Duke Street and Hunter Street which is just across the street from Tennent Caledonians *'Ladywell'* brewery.

The Overdale Bar wasn't one of the most salubrious public houses in Glasgow and was frequented by the inhabitants of the Great Eastern Hotel.

Don't be misled by the grand title, this was never a hotel, it had been built for use as a cotton mill in 1849 and was converted into a hostel for homeless workers in 1907.

At the time of this incident it still housed the homeless, few if any of whom could've been described as being workers.

Anyway, I sought out the paperwork relative to Robert's case and on reading it thought that perhaps the cops had locked up the wrong person.

Apparently the big fellow had been working behind the bar when a drunk man who lived in the *'Great E'* as it was known to the police in the area demanded more drink from Robert which he'd pay for when his Giro arrived a few days later.

Robert of course refused; the man continued to demand the drink and berated the big fellow for his constant refusal to serve him more drink.

Besides, the man was drunk and it's an offence to sell alcohol to a drunk person. (That must be the most unheeded law in this country)

The matter came to a head with the drunk smashing a pint tumbler and throwing it at Robert's head. How he missed, I don't know. Roberts head was, like the rest of his body, enormous.

Luckily the missile didn't find its target and the male made a dash for the exit onto Hunter Street.

He never made it; Robert caught hold of the creature and threw him bodily from the bar out into the street.

I think though, with the benefit of hindsight perhaps Robert should have taken the precaution of having the door opened first.

Police were summoned and Robert was arrested.

It wasn't ever going to be my enquiry and had already been allocated to a very strait-laced Detective Constable Willie R.

I asked him if he'd mind me speaking to the prisoner, it wasn't the done thing to intrude so I gave Willie his place and asked his permission first.

He gave me the OK and I made my way to the uniform area where I saw the duty Inspector, I can't remember his surname but he was called Alistair and was a very approachable wee man.

I asked to speak to Robert in his cell and was met with the question: *"Do you know him?"*

When told that we'd known each other for years, the Inspector replied that he also knew Robert.

Given all the circumstances of the assault I felt that if any case was reported to the Fiscal, it could have been dealt with other than by the means of a custody report.

It wasn't a particularly bad assault on the drunk and Robert had a fixed address which was more than the drunk had.

It also occurred to me; shouldn't he be locked up too? He had after all thrown a smashed beer glass at the publican's head.

I put it to the Inspector that perhaps Robert could be released and a case reported for consideration by the Fiscal at a later date.

"Yes" was the reply, *"the circumstances don't merit a custody case"*.

I was despatched to the C.I.D. general office to ask Willie R if he would mind calling in to see the duty officer at his convenience.

I told him what had transpired, Willie wasn't at all pleased with me but in all truth I didn't feel as though I'd done anything wrong.

Robert was released and I brought him along to the general office where he was given a cup of coffee to settle his nerves, the poor guy was shaking like a leaf. He'd never even been inside a police cell before in his life. He also had one of my Henri Winterman half corona cigars along with his coffee.

The cigar may actually have been smoked to disguise the foul tasting machine dispensed *'coffee'*.

I may be a bastard but what had been done there was wrong, there's a line that even I wouldn't cross.

Robert's older, uglier and even bigger brother Wullie F who I believe was a taxi driver was summoned and soon appeared at the office to collect Robert.

Wee Willie R was furious with me as he thought I'd pulled strings to get a friend out of trouble, it was never like that.

I didn't even ask if it ever went to trial or what the outcome was, it wasn't my concern.

What I had done was to establish even better relations with a very fruitful line of contacts. Word of my actions regarding Robert had got out amongst the taxi drivers and some were now speaking to me on a regular basis and filling my head with knowledge.

From venturing into the taxi office as a young constable, chancing my arm whilst scrounging a hot cup of tea and a heat from the gas fire. I now had *'eyes and ears'* all over the city of Glasgow.

One good turn deserves another.

Before I forget, if you cast your mind back to the chapter entitled *'Frankie'* you may recall I put the *'housebreaker'* into a police vehicle prior to the pub manager arriving.

That was because the manager was *'big Robert'* and I quite liked Frankie too.

The Nerston Strangler

When I retired from Strathclyde Police and decided to record the recollections of my service in book form I also resolved to make it as accurate a document as was humanly possible. There may be an error here and there, but nothing intentional.

It has also provided me with the platform to wreak revenge on some of those who were proven not to be my friends and if given the opportunity would have attempted to harm me or my career, insignificant as it was.

One such person first came to my notice when I was still a very junior uniformed constable working out of the old Eastern Division Headquarters building in Tobago Street which is in the Calton area of Glasgow and only a stones throw from 'The Barras Market' and Glasgow Cross.

He had a bit more service than me and I believe considered me to be a bit of an upstart with too much to say for myself.

I shall refer to him as 'A' in order to make it easier for him to recognise who it is I am alluding to.

His whole world revolved around strong drink, whisky in particular and to this day I believe he and one other person were responsible for the removal of a bottle of whisky from my clothing locker at London Road police office. (Referred to in my first book *Greenshields - A Glasgow Cop*).

The police were most certainly not all *'good guys'*.

I got on well with most of the cops on my uniform shift; they were all pretty decent individuals. We played football together, had social evenings and all the things that work colleagues do when not actually working.

One colleague, *'big Jock Gillespie'* (the arch-enemy of Lumpy Heid from book 1) and I hit it off well as he and I had a hobby in common.

We were both avid trout fishermen, very often we would take ourselves off to a loch or river in his native Ayrshire where this barbarian would set up three or four rods all baited with worms and sit back and wait for the fish to hook themselves.

I, on the other hand was a *'purist'*. I caught my fish using a fly rod.

We were the odd couple.

Jock was a good man to know, he had relations in Ayrshire who farmed land bordering the river Stinchar and using those family connections managed to obtain permission for us to fish the river for trout and grayling if we promised not to attempt to take any of their prized salmon.

We solemnly promised not to touch the salmon, I was lying; my fingers were crossed behind my back when making that solemn pledge. I would quite happily kill anything I caught.

It was late November and what little daylight there was would have to be fully utilised.

Just one wee drawback, our senior sergeant John McK. was retiring after completing thirty years with the police and had arranged his *'payoff'* for the evening before Jock and I were to fish the Stinchar.

A dilemma, John was a really decent man and it would have been downright rude of us not to attend his farewell do, but a day on the Stinchar was not to be given up lightly.

The solution was simple, we would do both.

Jock asked me to take my car to the Cottage Bar in Abercromby Street, Bridgeton where the payoff was to be held as he drank more than I did.

I could have a beer and be happy with that; he could take a drink and still get home safely. Jock had obtained permission for the fishing trip so I was happy with the deal.

There was however a fly in the ointment.

'A', who lived in the same town as Jock and myself had somehow got to hear I was taking my car into Glasgow and wasn't slow to ask if he could travel with us. I would much rather not have had to pick him up but it would've been very rude of me not to do so. Had he been driving I don't think he would have even considered asking if I wanted a lift.

We arrived at the pub about seven thirty that evening and were greeted by the retiring sergeant.

He ushered Jock, 'A' and myself to the bar and told us to order what we wished as the bar would be free all evening; it wasn't to cost us a penny.

I was only to have a beer, that was the agreement and it was to be a free bar!

I think perhaps Jock had prior knowledge of that situation.

I sat in the bar nursing my beer and listening to the stories being related by and about Sergeant John.

I believe he may have been a bit of a character in his day, my earliest recollection of John was when I was a young probationary constable seeing him walking down London road from Tobago Street police office towards the Barras Market with a large bin-bag under his arm and returning along the same street about an hour later with the now bulging bag slung over his shoulder. It would have been filled with goodies *'donated'* by stall-holders. If they wanted a quiet life then there was a price to pay and John exacted that price.

I didn't see any of the Barras traders at his pay-off, strangely enough. .

The evening wore on and just after ten o'clock I reminded Jock of the fishing trip in the morning.

I could see he was torn between staying on and coming with me.

My tactics were simple, *'drink up and come now or you'll be getting the bus home'*

It was a bitterly cold night and the rain was turning to sleet, Jock wasn't for standing at a bus stop in Abercromby Street, Bridgeton when he could be delivered to his own door.

I sought out *'A'* to let him know we were leaving within a few minutes, he could do what he wanted but we were going anyway.

He was seated alone at a table near to the toilet door, the table in front of him was littered with empty whisky glasses and I saw at least ten glasses still containing what was obviously the demon drink, electric soup.

He was taking full advantage of the free bar and just making a pig of himself.

I thought I'd be as well going for a pee as I'd no doubt be bursting for one by the time I got home.

I'd only been gone from the bar for a couple of minutes, I've only got a half-pint bladder and I'd had a pint of beer. *'A'* was standing with Jock at the table waiting for me to return. I glanced at the table-top; all the glasses were now empty.

'A' had a really surly look on his face; it was time to get him home.

Jock and I thanked Sergeant John for his hospitality and wished him well in his retirement. *'A'* wasn't speaking as we left the party.

My car was parked just behind the pub which was just as well because the wind was bitterly cold and the sleet was falling even heavier now.

Jock sat in the front passenger seat whilst 'A' sat directly behind me.

He hadn't uttered a word all the way from the pub in Bridgeton, through Dalmarnock, Rutherglen, Cathkin and onto the East Kilbride Road which was now white with snow and was being driven by the bitingly cold wind.

As we reached the crest of the hill at Nerston (from where, on a clear day almost the whole of the city of Glasgow can be viewed) just outside East Kilbride, 'A' suddenly shouted out: *"You bastard! You know! You bastard! You know!"* and gripped me around the throat with both hands from behind.

I struggled to breathe and keep control of the car which was by this time careering all over the snow covered carriageway.

Jock reached over into the rear of the car and pulled the enraged 'A' away from me.

I managed to steer the vehicle into a large lay-bye where I stopped to recover my breath. Jock got out of the car, opened the rear passenger door and was in the act of pulling the *'strangler'* from his seat when I asked him what he was doing.

'Leave the bastard here' was his reply.

As much as I would've loved to accede to his suggestion, I had to say *'no, he'll die if we leave him here'*.

Jock pushed 'A' back into the vehicle and we drove off towards his home which was only about another five minutes drive from the lay-bye.

It was now about eleven o'clock in the evening and 'A's' living room light was still lit.

His wife would no doubt be nursing her wrath; she could be left to deal with the inebriate.

Jock and I assisted him from the back seat and almost carried him along his quite lengthy garden path towards the now open front door where his good lady stood arms folded. (I wonder how many of us have witnessed a similar sight over the years?)

"What do you mean by bringing my husband home in that condition?" she bawled at us.

Jock and I just took off back along the path towards the car and safety.

As we ran for our lives I thought to myself we should have left the bugger in the lay-bye.

Did the woman really think we'd held her husband down and forced the drink into his mouth?

She must have seen him in that condition more than just a few times.

The following week we were back at work and on the night-shift.

Jock had lost no time in letting the others on the shift know of the incident involving *the Nerston strangler*.

'A' professed to have no recollection of the strangling incident and apologised profusely. I have my doubts. He was never to be a passenger in my car again.

Not long afterwards I moved on and became a C.I.D. officer; we had very little contact over the following years from that time on as I'd been transferred elsewhere. He retired shortly before I did.

A year or so later I was sitting in a chair at my favourite barbers shop in the old village part of East Kilbride having my now greying beard trimmed and discussing this new found hobby of writing with barber *John* who was aware I was writing a book of recollections.

John asked if I knew of a man by the name of 'A' who also frequented this shop. He said he'd worked with me in the *East* many years before.

'A' wondered to John the barber if he would by any chance get a mention in my book.

Well, Nerston strangler you wanted it!

The cameraman

Another routine day at the office, I smiled across the room at D/constable St.... he visibly cringed. This young detective had taken a few beatings in court because of my tactics but all credit to him; he still came back for more of the same.

Maybe he was simply punch drunk by this stage.

The C.I.D Clerk, Ian Harvey, was sitting quietly at his desk doing his admin tasks; I decided to leave him alone as I'd already learned not to get on his wrong side. He kept some real horror bags of enquiries in his bottom drawer just waiting for some poor unsuspecting fool to step out of line.

I'd been there and certainly didn't want another one fired in my direction.

I'd need to find something to do very soon or D/constable St... would no doubt be coerced into joining me in a hunting party which could often end in tears. With him in tears that is.

The door to the general office opened and in came a uniformed sergeant, Brian McK. a thoroughly decent wee man.

Brian approached Ian, the Clerk and spoke with him for a couple of minutes.

Ian looked over at me, smiled and pointed a finger in my direction.

The sergeant walked towards me.

My boredom was about to be ended for a few days.

Brian told me he had an uncle who owned a chemists shop on Alexandra Parade and some female members of staff there had come across photographs which had been developed at the request of a customer.

The snap-shots were of naked young females aged approximately 12 to 15 years, all appeared to be taking a bath.

Brian asked me if I would investigate the matter.

To be honest I'd never had to make enquiry into anything remotely similar but it was in the *'not too hard to solve'* category.

The customers name and address were obviously known as they were kept along with the request to have the film developed.

I looked over to D/Constable St..., his head went down onto the desk and I'm sure I heard the sound of sobbing.

Having attempted to reassure the poor sod that all was well and he wouldn't be the subject of yet another complaint, I told him what the nature of the enquiry was.

He was onto his feet and had his jacket on in an instant.

Maybe, just maybe, I wasn't such a bad lad after all.

We made our way to the shop which if my memory serves me correctly was near to the junction of Armadale Street and Alexandra Parade.

The owner was there, a middle aged man with greying hair along with two female members of staff.

My colleague and I identified ourselves to them and were directed to the back-shop where we were shown a collection of what appeared to be holiday snaps until we got to the last ten or so photographs.

These were the ones which had caused alarm.

They all showed naked teenage girls bathing, sometimes two in the bath together sometimes only one.

There were perhaps four or five different females involved and it was certainly the same bathroom as the décor hadn't changed in any of the photographs.

The customer was due to call for his holiday snaps about 2pm that day, we would be there to. If he turned up a bit early then the staff would delay him thus giving us time to attend.

I took possession of the photos and returned to the police office where they were shown to the Det/Superintendent who to my utter surprise and dismay just smiled and shook his head before walking away.

It is hard to believe, but I swear to God that is exactly what occurred.

I was shocked by his attitude; absolutely anything could have been happening to those children.

A couple of detectives sidled over to my desk; they wanted a look at the images. They were to be disappointed, I put them into my jacket pocket and as time was wearing on Det/constable St... and I made our way back to Alexandra Parade and the chemists shop.

We sat in the back-shop and waited patiently for the male to call for his holiday snaps. I'd already placed the indecent images with the rest of his photographs.

About twenty minutes after two o'clock the chemist came into the rear of the shop and said: *"That's him, he's here".*

We watched as this man who looked to be into his seventies paid for the processing, took possession of his property and left the shop.

We followed him out onto the footway, he'd stopped a few yards away from us and was leafing through the photographs and was totally oblivious to our presence until I spoke to him.

He knew instantly why we were there, the shocked expression on his face said it all.

I took the package of photographs from his grasp and told him he was being detained as suspect for being in possession of indecent images of children.

He didn't say a word.

Having already established his identity and home address from the chemist we took him directly to London Road police office for interview.

During that interview I laid the images out on a table and asked the elderly man to account for his possession of them.

His explanation was simple and straightforward, he allowed teenage girls who were truanting from a local secondary school to use his flat as a refuge during school hours. The price they had to pay for this refuge was to allow him to photograph them naked in his bath. He alleged that he never touched any of the children.

Were there any other photographs of children in his possession?

"Aye, a few hundred", was his reply.

How long has this been going on?

"About thirty years".

I requested he give us access to his flat for the purpose of searching it, if he refused me permission I would obtain a search warrant from Glasgow Sheriff Court that day and make the search anyway.

He agreed to allow the search without warrant.

There was no shortage of volunteers to assist us for some strange reason.

I chose two of the less voyeuristic detectives to accompany us to the man's flat which was only about five minutes walk from the chemists shop.

It was a quite well furnished flat consisting of a living-room, bedroom and bathroom.

The bathroom was without doubt the one where the children had been photographed, the décor being identical with the décor in the photos.

I asked where the other snaps could be located and a sideboard consisting of three drawers in the living-room was indicated,

One of my colleagues opened the top drawer and found only cutlery and table mats etc.

The second and third drawers both contained literally hundreds of images of naked girls, some of the pictures were obviously years old and were yellowing with age, and some had been taken with an 'Instamatic' camera which you may recall printed the picture on the spot.

Many others bore serial numbers on the rear thus showing they had been processed by a photographic laboratory.

We took possession of whatever camera equipment was to hand and also notebooks containing lists of girls' names some with addresses and some with telephone numbers noted alongside them.

I had already decided to have this man held in custody for an appearance at Glasgow Sheriff Court the following day. I would return to the police office and prepare a report for the Procurator Fiscal's attention and ask that he be remanded in custody whilst I attempted to trace the females involved.

It wasn't going to be too difficult to trace his most recent victims but the earlier ones might prove to be a bit more difficult.

I jotted a case down on paper simply showing that a crime had been committed and further enquiry would be required.

That really was all the Fiscal wanted to know at that point; elaboration of the circumstances surrounding the matter could follow later.

I also elected to present my report to a Depute Fiscal personally at the case reception in the morning and hope the Depute on duty was female.

The following day I got my wish and the young lady Depute was suitably appalled after reading the case and viewing some of the images I'd taken with me to hopefully bolster my plea for a remand.

The lady said she was glad that she and her family lived in the West End and not the East where this awful thing had occurred.

On my return to the office I began the search for the females involved.

I telephoned the numbers noted alongside girls names and spoke with adults who answered the calls.

I asked if they had a female child or children at a school in Dennistoun or nearby and if there was a problem with truanting.

I arranged to call at their homes and explained the problem in full.

The addresses of the girls without telephone numbers were also visited and very soon all of the girls in the latest photographs were identified.

There may well have been some chastened young ladies in the East end of Glasgow at that time.

The Fiscal I'd dealt with had asked to be kept updated on the progress or otherwise of the enquiry and when contacted by me the day before the accused was due to re-appear in court, this was the hearing to decide whether he would be further remanded or released pending trial, she said the defence agent had offered a plea of guilty to the original charge concerning possession of indecent images of children.

The young lady Fiscal admitted to me she had sought advice from a senior colleague in her office regarding whether to accept the offer or go to trial later. She had been advised to accept the guilty plea as the penalty would more than likely be same for 5 charges or 25.

There would be absolutely no point in me protesting, the matter was entirely out of my hands.

The Procurator Fiscal's decision is final.

Only the original charge could be referred to in court, the other as yet unproved allegations could not even be mentioned.

I felt cheated.

It was made worse later when I heard what the sentence was.

This dirty old man, this danger to youngsters, had been warned as to his future conduct and advised to move to another part of the City.

Perhaps he moved to the West End of Glasgow where the Fiscal said she lived.

P.S. Want to buy some naughty pictures?

It wisnae me

Some years ago, just a few, when I was a young detective working out of London Road police office I was tasked with investigating the theft of tools from a van which had been parked outside a row of semi-derelict shops on Gallowgate near to its junction with Fielden Street.

The row was very run down and had consisted of a pub, the name of which escapes me at present, a newsagent/tobacconist, a grocer cum off licence, a chippie and of course the inevitable bookies shop.

I believe the building was owned by Glasgow City Council who had in their wisdom decided to renovate the property before it fell down.

Hence the reason for the presence of a whole gang of tradesmen being there at that time.

The theft had reportedly been discovered the driver of the van, a joiner who had returned to his vehicle after a lunch break.

To his dismay he saw the rear doors had been forced open and a large canvas bag which contained the tools of his trade was missing from the back of the van.

He was, to say the least, distraught. Being a self employed journeyman joiner he was now unable to pursue his livelihood.

It still being lunchtime, there were hordes of children about as the local secondary school, St Mungo's Academy is situated almost directly behind the row of shops and there being a chip shop the children would gather there to dine on such delicacies as chips and curry sauce, greasy hamburgers or even that Glasgow speciality, the deep fried chocolate Mars Bar.

Questions were asked of the children who were milling around, most of course saw or heard nothing; this was the East End after all.

However, two young girls did respond to the irate joiner by telling him they had seen a boy taking a large bag from the rear of a van parked outside the now derelict pub before making off towards the Barrowfield housing estate which is only about five minutes walk from the shops or two minutes if you are running.

Instead of making his way directly to the police office which is itself located at the other end of Fielden Street from where the incident occurred, the ex-joiner tied the rear doors shut with a piece of string and drove his vehicle the very short along Gallowgate to Fielden Street and turned left onto Camlachie Street which leads directly into the Barrowfield through a dingy 1950's style industrial estate.

I think if the now fuming man had caught up with the felon there may have been a re-enactment of the crucifixion scene taking place in the Barrowfield.

The man was very cross.

Having drawn a blank, he now made his way to London Road office where I was next in line for an enquiry.

The allocation of work was a lottery; you just had to take what came in turn.

I watched as the great man, the C.I.D Clerk Ian Harvey, rose from his desk and approached the enquiries window where he took a report from the joiner. I cringed as Ian turned and smiled in my direction.

This was to be my enquiry.

Ushering the man over to my desk and asking him to take a seat opposite me, I went through the motions and tried to appear interested in his tale of misfortune but had already secretly written it off in my head as being in the *'too hard to solve'* category, I asked if he'd taken a note of the wee girl's names, the ones who'd seen the thief make off.

Of course the man didn't think to do so at the time, he just wanted his tools returned. I could understand that.

There was no insurance cover for his tools and the cost of replacing them was beyond his financial capability.

The very least I could do was make some effort, do a bit of enquiry to maybe salve my own conscience a bit.

I assured the man I would make diligent enquiries and get back to him with whatever information I could discover. Little consolation for a man who had just lost the means of earning a living.

He left the building with a big black cloud hovering over his head.

I went back to my desk and had another look at the Glasgow Herald crossword, fumbled about in my pockets searching for a ten pence piece to buy yet another cup of coffee and felt a burning sensation in the back of my head.

Have you ever had the feeling someone was looking at you?

I raised my eyes from the newspaper and looked across the office to Ian's desk; he was giving me one of his *'get off your arse'* looks.

Not a man to cross, he didn't have to say anything, the look was enough.

Getting to my feet and petulantly pulling my Ralph Slater suit jacket on I dared to give him a dirty look which he saw.

Ian was on his feet and making for my desk in a second, not quickly enough, I was off and out of the general office before he could inflict any damage to my handsome face.

There being no other detective constables in the office at that time for one reason or another, I would have to find myself a neighbour elsewhere.

The door to the Det/Sergeants' room was lying open so I had a look inside; a sergeant nicknamed *'the panto queen'* was seated at his desk.

He would do.

This was a man who couldn't work late one evening on a murder enquiry because he had two tickets for the ballet. He is also the person to whom I referred in the opening chapter of book two as the officer who had *'diked'* the Rab Black enquiry.

I asked if he was available to accompany me into Barrowfield, the land that time forgot as I had an enquiry there and there were no other detectives in the office.

There was no way he wanted to leave his warm, comfortable office to enter extremely unfriendly territory but neither could he refuse my request as he was actually reading his newspaper when I asked the question.

'No, I'm too busy,' wasn't an option, he had to agree to go with me.

Going into Barrowfield on my own was unthinkable. I would've been captured, roasted on a spit and eaten. Even the uniformed cops, the *'beatmen'*, patrolled the area in twos.

'Hostile' is possibly the best word to describe some of the inhabitants.

'Neanderthal' also springs to mind.

I explained to the *'panto queen'* what had occurred and his facial expression showed he had as much interest in the enquiry as I had but his Daily Telegraph fashion page would have to wait, Duty called.

I reasoned if the thief had made his way along Gallowgate and Camlachie Street towards Barrowfield he would more likely than not be a *'Barrowfielder'* himself.

Sticking my head round the door to ensure the coast was clear and Ian the C.I.D clerk wasn't lying in wait for me in the corridor I quickly fled out of the rear door into the yard at the back of the building to where my getaway car was waiting. The shabby brown coloured Austin Maestro with a detachable gear lever. State of the art police vehicle my arse. There was always a rush in the morning to grab a set of keys; the last set to be taken off their hook was for a certain Maestro.

It was better than nothing, well almost...

A set of joinery tools would be easily disposed of either to a resetter in the Barrowfield or at the Barras market the following weekend or perhaps at the Briggait market which was located behind the High Court building in Saltmarket. The Briggait market was open most days and was renowned throughout the city for the sale of stolen property.

I would concentrate on the Barrowfield first and if there was no joy to be had there I'd have to look further afield.

Panto queen insisted that I drive the damned thing as it was beneath his dignity to pilot such a lowly vehicle. Sorry sir, the Daimler appears to be taken already!!!!

It is only about two minutes drive from London Road police office to Barrowfield, It is also like entering a time warp, women with rollers in their hair and wearing headscarves, taking their washing to the *'steamie'*.

Flats which had been renovated and converted to *'all electric'* now had open coal fires again having been re-converted by the inhabitants to the old style.

Quite right too, you can't boil a kettle on an electric fire can you?

I drove the car to the top end of Stamford Street and stopped at the corner of *'big Dalserf Street'* where I got out.

No victims to be seen, no hostages to be taken, the street was almost deserted. If there were no boys about then I would take a female into *'custody'* instead.

I got back into the car and drove down to *'wee Dalserf Street'* where we saw an *'almost female'* relative of the McK.. family standing outside her close.

She would suffice in the absence of her male counterparts.

This girl had been the subject of a body search at London Road police office a couple of weeks earlier and the female turnkey who had done the searching was heard to remark later: *"she is filthy, her pants are caked with shit"*.

Not quite the girl you would want to take home to your mother.

She obviously recognised the car as being a C.I.D. vehicle then saw me driving it. This human dung beetle turned and ran into the close, no luck, the door at the back of the close was locked and I had her trapped.

Perhaps a wee trip to the office for another body search for controlled drugs was called for. I loved the powers contained in the Misuse of Drugs Act 1971. Legislation just made to be used and abused.

I hoped the same female turnkey wasn't on duty or I'd receive an ear-bashing from her when she saw who the latest customer would be.

The young lady had possibly missed a few days at her *'finishing school'* in Geneva as she asked very impolitely: *"What the fuck dae you want noo Greenshields?"*

It was quickly pointed out that to her I would always be *'Mr Greenshields sir'* and she should keep a civil tongue her head.

Placing her very gently headfirst into the rear of the car beside my posh sergeant who wasn't over the moon with me by now, I returned towards the police office.

Driving along Barrowfield Street which runs along the rear of the office, I was pleased to hear her say: *"Stoap the motor Mr Greenshields, whit is ye waant tae know?"* She didn't actually sound the letter *'t'* in motor, it came out something like mo-urr.

It may have been my boyish good looks and devil-may care charm that won the ladies heart, or perhaps not. She might just have been concealing a dark secret inside her pants.

The question was simple: *"Who stole the toolbag from the van in Gallowgate this morning and where is it now?"*

This little bitch was a member of an extended family of criminals in Barrowfield who were into every type of petty crime imaginable.

There was no doubt in my mind the answer would be found inside her head as surely as something nasty would be found in her knickers.

She sat silently looking out of the car window for a minute or so then asked if she would be allowed to go if I was told where to find the stolen property.

The deal was never going to be that simple, she would remain in a detention room whilst the Det/Sergeant and I recovered the toolbag. Then and only then would she be released without being strip searched, there would of course be a cursory search to ensure there were no weapons or anything harmful concealed about her smelly little body.

The deal was done.

There was no way she would say who had actually done the deed which to my mind anyway tended to show it was either one of her thieving junkie brothers or one of her equally low life cousins who was responsible.

The bag and its contents had been sold almost immediately to a man who lived in the bottom flat right, in a block of flats in Camlachie Street near to Stamford Street.

If we were quick the property may still be found in his possession.

I contacted the two Barrowfield beat cops by radio and after picking them up from their usual hiding place at Jimmy Frears yard on London Road we then made our way to the flat. If there were any problems encountered in gaining entry to the premises I would simply leave the uniformed cops there and attend at a local Justice of the Peace to obtain a search warrant.

The sergeant just let me get on with it, I was in my element now.

As happy as a pig in shit!

I knocked loudly on the front door to the ground floor flat, the sergeant by my side whilst the uniforms each took up a position at the front and rear.

A voice from within called out: *"Maw, it's the polis at the door."*

I knocked again, a couple of minutes passed and still the door remained shut.

The sound of something being dragged across the floor could be heard then the closing of a door before a few more seconds elapsed and the front door was opened by a Barrowfield belle, a woman of about forty years of age who looked to be about sixty or more.

The Avon Lady had obviously failed to call that week. She'd probably been held up and robbed. I wont say *'mugged'*, I detest that expression.

I showed her my warrant card but I think she may have suspected we weren't Mormon missionaries seeking converts in the East End of Glasgow. There were no formal introductions.

Her husband had apparently gone out a short time before we arrived, no matter. The only people in the house were this beauty and a streetwise boy of about twelve years.

We weren't being invited in so I asked if we might come in for a chat.

The standard reply was fired straight back at me: *"Huv ye goat a warrant?"*

I replied: *"No, but I'll get one in less than half an hour and if I find what I'm looking for in your house I'll lock both of you up, you and your ugly child."*

She hesitated then motioned us forward into the flat. I noticed that my shoes were sticking to the carpet as I walked along the hallway towards her living room.

Having briefly explained why we had called, (I think perhaps she already knew) but I had to go through the motions anyway.

I asked if there was a toolbag in the house, the woman looked sheepishly at me and said: *"my man's."* She pointed to the hall and continued: *"It's in the cupboard."*

Surprise, surprise, it was a large canvas bag full of joinery tools. I had to ask: *"Is your man a joiner?"*

"Naw" was the not unexpected reply.

Removing the bag from the cupboard I said: *"tell him to come to the police office, I would like a word with him."*

Needless to say the very relieved joiner got his tools back and hopefully didn't *'lose'* them again, the thief was never caught but the resetter from Camlachie Street was later fined at Glasgow District Court aka *'the Palais de Justice'* for his part in the incident.

He wasn't a happy man.

I had no further dealings with him before taking leave of my beloved East and few months later I moved on to pastures new, Strathclyde Police Drugs Squad at the Force Headquarters in Pitt Street, Glasgow.

I can honestly say I never gave him another thought until one day on turning up for a late shift at the squad offices I was told to report to a Chief Inspector at the Complaints and Discipline Section who wished to speak to me regarding a complaint from a member of the public.

This baffled me, I hadn't been up to anything, certainly no planting of drugs, no throw-away lines or gratuitous violence when dealing with the 'neds', nothing came to mind.

The Chief Inspector was based on the second floor of the building, this was where the Inquisition lived, the men in grey suits and rubber heels.

A man with a face like a City Bakeries Halloween cake ushered me into his room which I noticed was very tidy, he must have had a lot of time on his hands; my desk was always littered with pieces of paper and the occasional beer bottle.

The scariest thing was the oil painting of the Grand Inquisitor himself, Torquemada, hanging on the wall. *(that bit's not true)*.

I was informed by the Chief Inspector that a letter of complaint had been received from a man who was alleging damage had been caused to his vehicle and the perpetrator was none other than myself.

I was mystified until shown the letter, it was from the resetter in Camlachie Street.

Revenge is a dish best served cold, he'd waited for a while then tried to cause me grief by making a malicious complaint about me.

I tried hard not to laugh on being shown a copy of the letter, the damage according to his account was to his *'looting van'* and his *'solictor'* had advised him to contact the police himself regarding my alleged involvement.

(Obviously his lawyer had given this complaint the arms length treatment.)

I think he actually meant his Luton van but then again he may have been correct in his description of the vehicle and its purpose.

This Chief Inspector may have smelled blood, mine. He asked me to give him a written account of my movements on the night in question.

My notebook was produced and clearly showed that there was no way I was anywhere near Barrowfield on that date.

We were actually engaged in an operation at a well known discotheque at Saltcoats in Ayrshire when I was supposed to be pushing his *'looting van'* down a hill in Camlachie Street in Glasgow.

To compound his bad luck with choice of date for the alleged offence, I'd been given a lift to work that evening by a Det/Sergeant, a friend of mine who lived close by me.

He had driven me to work, spent the rest of the night along with myself and the rest of the team raiding the disco for drugs, successfully I might add, Subsequently searching a house in Johnstone, Renfrewshire occupied by a man who'd been found within the toilets at the club in possession of a load of Ecstasy tablets and about 5 o'clock the following morning, long after I was supposed to have done this misdeed I was dropped off outside my home by my friend.

I was totally alibied from start to finish.

Having had to prove my innocence and shown the allegation to be malicious, I wanted the police, my employer, to take some action against this vengeful little creature..

Nothing was done.

Well, it is said that the world turns slowly, I believe he was found with quite a substantial amount of drugs in his possession a couple of years later.

The operative words being, Revenge, dish and cold.

No, I wasn't there either.

Cannabis factory in Battlefield

Although based in Castlemilk for a time and not really meant to be foraging outside of its boundaries my partner D/C. M and myself would sometimes stray into Aikenhead Road police office territory when we were at a loose end.

It didn't happen very often but we did *'poach'* there occasionally.

M had been in the South for a while and knew quite a lot people there, Every now and then he would receive information regarding drug dealing or whatever and if we weren't too busy in our own patch we would steal across the sub-divisional boundary and take the necessary action without first notifying anyone at the local H.Q.

The hierarchy there wouldn't bother overmuch as to who was doing the deeds just so long as there were detections showing up in their statistics every month. It's just a numbers game after all.

M liked to do *'drugs turns'*, I'd just done five years in the Drugs Squad and had seen enough of the stuff to last me a lifetime.

However, I could still be talked into going along, albeit quite reluctantly now. Changed days indeed.

He told me about an alleged Cannabis factory which was reported to be operating from a third floor flat in Battlefield Avenue not far from Langside College and the Victoria Infirmary on the south side of the city.

To be truthful, I was never much interested in *'cannabis turns'*, they seemed to me to be more bother than they were worth. That's only my personal opinion. I was much more interested in powders, L.S.D and Ecstasy tablets.

They really are *'the business'*.

The search warrant had already been applied for and would no doubt be granted before too long.

I suggested we take the opportunity to dress down to casual wear and have a look at the place before the big day as he hadn't even reconnoitred the area yet.

It wouldn't look too clever on our part if we turned up at the building and couldn't get in because there was a controlled entry system in operation.

Was the door to the flat strengthened in some way so as to prevent anyone forcing entry, was there a dog, how many persons could we expect to find in the flat?

Nothing had been thought through, it was to have been a hit and hope situation.

Not remotely professional.

We made our way to Battlefield Avenue about 7a.m. the following day in our old battered and clapped out Castlemilk C.I.D Ford Escort. I parked the car in nearby Brisbane Street, M and I made our way on foot the short distance to the subject address and found on our arrival there that was no door entry system at the close-mouth. That helped the cause enormously !!

The door to the subject address itself was of solid wood construction and would take a sledgehammer to remove it from its hinges. That could be arranged; I always liked that bit of the job.

No spy hole on the door and only two locks, one Yale type and one mortise.

It was agreed that six bodies would be sufficient for this job and if a female cop was required later, we'd request one to attend from Aikenhead Road police office.

Tuesday was the day selected for our visit as it was normally a quiet day with regards to crime, later in the week and week-ends were out of the question. They could be quite busy times.

We gathered at Castlemilk office at 7a.m. on the appointed day, the plain-clothes squad from Aikenhead Road were briefed as to the plan, such as it was and off we went.

It was a piece of cake. I knocked on the door to the flat which was opened almost immediately by a small, thin female who was probably only about 20 years of age. She was by no means pretty; in fact I would say she was extremely plain with eyes too big for her face. She looked like a frog. If this female was waiting for a handsome prince to come along and kiss her so that she could become a beautiful princess, the lady will still be a frog today.

M told her who we were and in we went.

The smell of growing cannabis was everywhere. I actually quite like the scent given off by it. There were only two rooms in the flat, the livingroom was off to the left and overlooked the street whilst the bedroom and a small bathroom were off to the right and looked out onto a back court.

Along with two of the *'plainers'*, I went into the livingroom where we found a man curled up in a makeshift bed. We woke him to give him the bad news.

Not best pleased would suffice to describe his mood when he realised he was in a wee bit of bother.

Signs of dope having been smoked in that room was everywhere, half smoked *'roaches'* in ashtrays, broken cigarettes and so on.

I really couldn't care less about people smoking cannabis in their own homes.

Cultivating it commercially is another matter entirely.

The other three in our party had found herbal cannabis growing inside a foil lined wooden construction in the bedroom. It was the classic hydroponics system with heatlamps, water and nutrients. He had about thirty plants at various stages of development in his *'garden shed'*.

No argument, no problem, he was detained. What could he say? *"How did that get there?"* or *"I've never noticed that before"*.

He had a *'black box'* fitted to his electricity meter to tamper with its recording mechanism. It's quite normal for cannabis growers to employ a box like that, saves a fortune on the bill.

Scottish Power would prosecute him for that too; it's the little things in life which make all the difference

I don't think D.I.Y. was his strongpoint; he'd knocked a big ragged hole in the wall from the electric meter cupboard in the hallway through to the bedroom where the cultivation had been found. Not just a hole big enough to allow a few cables through but one capable of being used as a serving hatch.

When I picture it in my mind's eye now, it may even have been a supporting wall he'd restructured.

The flat itself, was sub-let from a Jewish businessman who had an *'office'* on Battlefield Road just around the corner from the flat.

Small world, it was my ex-friend Michael the brothel keeper who'd caused me a bit of grief earlier. He gets a mention in book 2.

I would not be getting in touch with him. The devious little shit.

The tedious bit now has to follow. The set-up has to be photographed in situ, sample leaves are taken from the plants to be analysed at the forensic laboratory and the whole thing has then to be dismantled and taken to a police office and stored in a cell because it is so bulky.

As I said, more bother than its worth. Give me powders to deal with any day.

After appearing at Glasgow Sheriff court and pleading not guilty to being concerned in the production of a controlled drug, the male was released pending trial. We hadn't bothered with his pet frog who, as I recall, was quite heavily pregnant at the time.

Months went by and I'd forgotten all about 'the big drugs raid'. I'd been working in my garden at home on my day off and had to call at the local Civic Amenity Site, we used to call them rubbish dumps before we became so politically correct.

Who should I come across but my green fingered friend from Battlefield, he was working there at the composting area. Makes sense I suppose, he was a bit of a gardener after all.

No luck, a warrant had been issued for his arrest because he'd failed to return to court and his citations were not served as they'd moved house without leaving a forwarding address. Not at all considerate. He and his wife had hopped it.

The man was less than pleased to see me and even less pleased when the local plod came to collect him.

I don't think it even went to trial.

I wonder if he and Mrs Frog ever spawned any wee tadpoles.

Certainly not sir!

I just love it when the bad guy suddenly appears right in front of you, it's as if he's saying, *"Here I am, come and get me"*. Or in Glasgow parlance, *"Here I'm are."* That could only come from a Weegie.

Det/Constable Stevens and I were driving out of the Barrowfield along Fielden Place towards Fielden Street after an abortive search for a victim, any victim would do. All Barrowfielders between the ages of 16 and 60 were fair game.

As far as we were concerned anyone even eating a pickle in Stamford Street after 1 p.m. was committing an offence punishable by imprisonment or worse.

Oh how I miss the Glasgow Corporation Consolidation (General Powers) Order confirmation act 1960.

Offences such as;

Throwing wet rags at a procession,

Beating your carpets after 6p.m.

Leaving a horse and cart unattended.

I actually charged some-one with that) could be levelled against the lieges and often were.

The Barrowfielders were lying low today.

Thinking that perhaps the Calton including the Barras area may have been a bit more fruitful we decided to try our luck there.

On reaching the junction of Fielden Place and Fielden Street we were held up momentarily by a vehicle travelling in the opposite direction i.e. into Barrowfield.

There were two men in the car which was an old red coloured Ford Escort, the front seat passenger was a local inhabitant nicknamed Mousey, pronounced moosey.

The driver was also very well known to my co-pilot Stevens and me, it was none other than the reptile mentioned in my second book in the chapter entitled *'Assault with intent to what?'* He was the one with the distinctive fair hair cut in a fringe just above his eyebrows.

He'd just made our day.

A catalogue of offences such as theft of motor vehicles, driving whilst disqualified, no driving licence and having no insurance had seen him handed a quite lengthy ban from driving for a period of five years and yet here he was again.

Right under our noses.

Mousey and he were deep in conversation as they drove in towards the scheme, both apparently oblivious to our presence. Nothing out of ten for observation as the C.I.D. cars were all very well known in the area.

Not exactly covert, Mousey and company would no doubt have been passengers in those vehicles at some time.

Our car was turned about, no hurry, no fuss, we'd seen all we required to see. Even if he disappeared into the warren of houses that made up the place and we couldn't locate him, a case would be reported to the Fiscal's Office anyway.

We drove back along Fielden Place; turned left along Frazer Street where Mousey lived then right into Law Street, how inappropriately named is that?

Mousey was seen standing at the door of the general store in Stamford Street, I wondered where his accomplice might be.

The red coloured Escort was parked at the bottom of wee Dalserf Street outside Toal's close. The last close in the street.

The reptile could have been calling on Toal who is Mousey's cousin or even in the store buying that days Herald or Financial Times.

We opted for the store after calling up the local control room to have a marked vehicle attend and take charge of the Escort. It would have to be checked out, with any luck it would be a stolen car.

There he was, coming from the shop and lighting up a cigarette, before he could do anything about it, we had him. No struggle unfortunately.

Mousey called out to us, shouting: *"that's f***ing out of order Greenshields."*

I reminded him quite firmly and politely that he should refer to me as *'Mr Greenshields, Sir'.*

Mousey was one of the more literate of his tribe, his vocabulary was impressive. Attempting to alibi his mate he said: *"Incidentally, by the way, he's been in ma hoose aw day."*

There's always a wee *'by the way'* in there isn't there?

The marked van had now turned up and our uniformed colleagues took charge of the Escort car. We could concentrate on this human louse.

A quick check of our prisoner revealed a small screwdriver in his jacket pocket and a few coins.

The screwdriver would more than likely be his *'ignition key'*. Escorts were notoriously easy to steal by simply inserting something resembling a key into the ignition barrel and giving it a turn.

Mouseys mother, Mary, a vision of loveliness, 5 feet 2 inches in height, grossly overweight with further rings of fat on her already existing fat, dirty tee shirt which bore the signs of at least a years food staining down her voluminous front, a black skirt which may have started life some other colour and stockings down around her ankles now came shambling along Law Street towards us from the direction of her home.

She glared at us and shouted: *"Whit the f**k are ye daen noo, leave the boy alane, he's no done nothing wrang."*

I really think she had a secret crush on me and wanted to have our love child.

Mary was playing hard to get, quite successfully I might add (by the way).

I just had to add those three little words because I'm a Weegie too and as such am entitled if not obliged to finish every sentence with those immortal words which if deleted from the English language would leave many a native Glaswegian bereft.

We bid a fond farewell to the Barrowfields own goddess and took our capture to London Road police office where he would be detained until the result of the vehicle check had been ascertained by our colleagues.

A cup of coffee and a frame of snooker would pass the time quite nicely.

The end of our shift was fast approaching and overtime beckoned.

All this enjoyment and being paid for it too.

I may even return to Frazer Street later on in the evening and serenade Mary from the street below her balcony.

Perhaps not, she may take me up on it.

As I'd hoped, the car had indeed been stolen, it'd been taken from Wishart Street at the rear of Glasgow Royal Infirmary earlier that same day.

I love it when a plan comes together.

This was a piece of cake, I wrote the case just as it had happened, no exaggerations or deviations from the true facts, some of those who know me will be choking, but I swear to God I told the truth, I really did, honest, would I tell a lie?

The dung-beetle was detained for an appearance at court the following day, our part was done, all we had to do now was await the inevitable citation to appear at court for his trial.

He never pleaded guilty to anything, he invariably went the distance, at public expense I may add.

He always received Legal Aid. A sore point with me, but I'll resist the urge to have another rant about lawyers.

The trial duly came around about three months later, it was called under Solemn Procedure in the Sheriff and Jury Court because of his previous convictions I believe.

I thought at the time it was a bit unusual for what were after all not the most serious of charges to be heard under Solemn Procedure but I wasn't complaining.

The penalties if he was found guilty could be greater than if heard under Summary Procedure by a Sheriff sitting alone.

I really cannot think of many instances before or after this where I've attended a trial and been so completely relaxed and confident of getting the correct result.

The only police witnesses cited for the trial were D/c Stevens and myself and for once this poor sod wouldn't be spit roasted by the defence because of me.

I think I may have shortened his life span by a few years.

But do I care, he never got the jail, did he?

I was called into court by the Usher and shown into the witness box.

I may have found it myself without his help, it was a large brown coloured wooden pulpit standing empty just inside the court.

The Depute Fiscal lead me through my evidence, I told it like it was, it was so easy. Nothing to worry about, nothing in the slightest bit *'iffy'*.

No need to change my pampers this time.

The Depute gave me a wee smile and sat down, job done!

The defence agent got to his feet and went through my evidence but I felt he already knew the game was up.

His gambit was to destroy my credibility in front of the jury:

"These are mostly Road Traffic offences, are they not, how long have you been a Traffic cop Mr Greenshields?"

"I've never been a traffic cop," was my reply, *"but I've reported many road traffic cases before this."*

"So you're not an expert on traffic cases?"

"I'm not saying I'm an expert in anything but I have reported many different offences over the years."

The defence agent came back with: *"So you're saying you're an experienced officer who's dealt with many different aspects of the law in your career, is that correct?"*

"Yes sir, that's correct."

"What about prostitutes, have you ever had any dealings with prostitutes?"

Putting on my best, totally aghast face I replied: *"Certainly not sir, I'm a married man!"*

He'd obviously thrown in the towel and was now just having fun; well two can play at that game.

The jury were sniggering amongst themselves, the Fiscal had his head in his hands and the defence agent was grinning from ear to ear.

The accused had obviously missed it and was looking blankly around him.

His Lordship, the Sheriff, was also trying hard not laugh, he said: *"Constable I think my learned friend was asking if you had dealings with prostitutes in your capacity as a police officer not in your personal life."*

The defence agent just looked at me, smiled and shook his head: *"no further questions"* and sat down.

There was never any doubt in my mind I'd get the result I wanted but when the verdict of guilty came back and the sentence of 2 years imprisonment was handed down I was ecstatic.

This cretin would be back, he simply didn't learn.

Billy, Willie and Brian

Billy, Willie and Brian, the three Musketeers, the scourge of deliverymen in Dennistoun, on Duke Street in particular. This team were for ever on the lookout for an unattended goods vehicle parked outside any of the shops or pubs on that main thoroughfare.

They were probably responsible for more thefts of goods in transit than the entire workforce at Glasgow Docks.

One of the trio would act as look-out, in Glasgow parlance *'keep the edge'* whilst the other two henchmen liberated whatever they could lay hands on before the vehicle driver and his mate returned.

Thoroughly rehearsed and honed to perfection over the years, they were rarely disturbed and were masters of the *'snatch and run'*.

Professional to the last, they had it all worked out. Grab a case of beer, a box of frozen chickens or whatever from the rear of a lorry and run off downhill towards the sanctuary afforded by the blocks maisonettes and multi-storeys located halfway between Duke Street and Gallowgate.

Once in amongst this warren they could disappear with little or no chance of being discovered.

They had access to any number of dwellings in there.

I often wonder how many of the free portions of chicken and chips, kebabs, fish suppers and curries I received from my shopkeeper friends in Duke Street had earlier been spirited away along Bluevale Street by these three desperados.

Had I actually been eating the proceeds of theft all that time?

My only real claim to putting one over on Billy successfully was when in response to a complaint from a priest, Father McDonald at St Anne's Catholic Church in Bluevale Street regarding his having windows broken on a regular basis, I decided one night to stand in a close at number 22 Bluevale Street across the street from the church about closing time and wait for the pubs to spill their customers out onto the street.

It always seemed to be quite late on in the evening when this malicious mischief occurred.

Logical, to my way of thinking anyway, some-one on his way home from the pub would put another brick through the church window and run off.

My neighbour and I waited quietly for about thirty minutes before we heard the sound of running feet, a crash and the sound of breaking glass coming from across the street.

We were out of the close in a second and there right in front of us was Billy.

Not another soul in sight, 'come to daddy, you're getting the jail'.

My neighbour being much quicker on foot than I was ran after the culprit and as Billy was full of beer, the chase was a short one.

We had our window remover in custody.

Next day when I was just coming on duty in the C.I.D. general office, I received a call from a uniformed Inspector to say that the priest, Father McDonald, wished to see me. Would I pay him a visit?

Why would he want to see me? I'm a White Anglo Saxon Protestant who supports a football team from the other side of the city.

His church may even fall down if I set foot inside it or I could be struck down by a bolt of lightning.

Being well earthed, wearing rubber soled shoes, I made my way there on foot as it was a lovely summers evening and the church is only about ten minute's walk from the police office.

The door to the church-house was opened by an elderly lady whom I took to be Mrs McDonald; I asked if her husband, Father McDonald was at home. A withering look greeted me, she turned silently on her heels and re-entered the house.

A couple of minutes elapsed before I heard a loud laugh come from inside, an elderly white haired man in dark clothing and wearing a dog-collar then appeared in the doorway.

In a very soft Western Isles accent he said: *"You'll be Willie the night shift constable?"*

"Come away in."

I was shown into a quite large living-room and seated on the couch in front of a coal fire.

He thanked me for putting a stop to the mindless vandalism, for the time being at least.

Unfortunately cretins like Billy will always come back, they are beyond salvation.

I wouldn't even try, they aren't worth the effort.

The old gent shook my hand and said: *"You'll have a half with me Willie?"*

I got the feeling he wasn't really asking, he was saying you WILL have a half with me.

Not a man to refuse and cause offence I accepted one or two wee tastes of a rather nice Single Malt whisky.

After a short stay I took my leave and reluctantly went back to work.

It was the start of a long night and drinking on an empty head isn't a good idea.

A few months after the incident with the window smashing I heard that Billy's mother had passed away, as fate would have it the funeral service was to be performed in the church in Bluevale Street. Billy's mother had been a parishioner of Father McDonald.

As Billy, Willie and Brian assisted in carrying the coffin from the hearse into the church, a bystander was heard to remark: "that's the first time I've seen those three carrying a box down Bluevale Street and they weren't running with it."

I met Billy in the Main Street, Cambuslang a couple of years ago; he owns a wee fancy goods shop there selling greetings cards and the like and claims to be a legitimate businessman now.

Aye right, so was Al Capone.

Scaffolding and soft brown leather

A n unlikely pairing you would think unless used for some strange nocturnal goings-on. However, the truth is the soot and grime stained stonework of Glasgow Cathedral was receiving a long overdue clean up.

Contractors had been brought in to scrape years of accumulated filth off this beautiful structure and to hopefully restore the stone to its original colour. Grey.

Why bother?

As access had to be gained to the very top of the Cathedral, its 13th century tower, the stone-cleaners had in turn hired a large quantity of tubular metal scaffolding from a company with premises in nearby Ballindalloch Drive in the north part of Dennistoun.

Prior to erection, I love that word, it brings back memories of my youth, the poles were stored on the roadway beside the building where the fairly recently built Museum of St Mungo now stands.

They were left there unattended for a few of days, from the close of work on Friday afternoon until Monday morning when the workers returned to the site.

For reasons best known to them the company tasked with the clean-up job had failed to provide any security personnel and as a result about fifty percent of the scaffolding which had been daubed by the owners with bright blue paint to assist with identification in the event of it being stolen had now gone.

The value of the missing property ran into tens of thousands of pounds.

The owners of the scaffolding were immediately informed of the theft; they in turn reported the matter to the police at the London Road office.

I, thankfully, missed the enquiry by a hairsbreadth; I'd just been allocated two reports of thefts by housebreaking which had also occurred over that particular week-end.

Both buildings violated had been used as business premises and were located next door to each other in St Andrews Street which is just off Saltmarket near to Glasgow Cross.

One was a wholesale warehouse used for storing and selling leather jackets and the other was a lawyer's office.

No need to guess which one of those two would receive my undivided attention.

You're correct; it wasn't ever going to be the lawyer.

The scaffolding enquiry was initially touted around to some supervisory officers but all declined as they, to a man and one woman who was almost a man, said they were far too busy.

I was about to make off and hide in the gymnasium toilet again, my 'safe-house' when my partner Joe was called over to the Clerks desk and handed the crime report.

My heart went out to him, I really felt sorry for the poor guy.

My backside, I was only glad to have avoided it myself.

Joe reluctantly took the green coloured paper form containing the details of the alleged crime from the C.I.D Clerk, Ian Harvey, a man not to be trifled with and trudged back to his desk where he sat across from me reading this horror story.

Given the value of the property stolen I felt that the matter should have been dealt with by a supervisory officer, that after all is what they receive an extra shilling a week for. Isn't it?

His normally florid complexion changed to a deep red and the poor sod was apoplectic.

Instead of recording the owner of the scaffolding as being the company in Ballindalloch Drive, the person who'd noted the complaint had mistakenly decided that the 'complainer' should be the Crown.

The Cathedral is maintained by Historic Scotland and is therefore the property of the Crown; he reasoned therefore, anything stolen from that place must also belong to the Crown.

Joes' head went down onto the desk and I distinctly heard him say,: "Aw f**k!"

I think the pubs in Joe's home town would be on the receiving end of a drinking frenzy later.

He liked a small aperitif of an evening.

I loved his reasoning; *'That's no theft, that's effing treason, somebody could hang for this'.*

The analogy between scaffold and hanging did occur to me at the time but I felt it best not to say anything which may upset the poor man any further.

Joe and I were going to be very busy boys for the foreseeable future.

I suggested we called at the Cathedral first as his enquiry was probably more pressing than mine.

Ian Harvey smiled and looked away, if I was a bastard, he was the master. I was only playing at it. I lifted the car keys from my desk and we headed off to investigate these heinous crimes.

I was the designated driver in our team as Joe was banned for life from ever driving police vehicles again. He'd allegedly committed a somewhat trivial offence a few years earlier and the head of the Traffic department, a former Gestapo officer, had decreed that Joe was to be forever again a pedestrian policeman.

Driving didn't bother me, except when I'd to drive the Austin Maestro which had a detachable gear lever.

It surely couldn't have passed an M.O.T. test?

We drove up Abercromby Street, along Duke Street onto High Street and stopped the car outside Glasgow Cathedral on Castle Street.

Joe and I sought out the site agent, we found him sitting in his portakabin at the rear of the building drinking tea and reading his morning paper, the *Daily Record.*

He didn't appear to be overly concerned that thousands of pounds worth of property had been stolen from his site but I suppose it wasn't really his problem as the scaffolding belonged to some-one else.

This man was the penny-pincher who'd failed to hire a night watchman to patrol the area just to save his employer a few shillings.

When asked about the presence of security personnel on site he merely shrugged his shoulders and said: *"there's nane."*

No C.C.T.V. cameras, nothing. The site was left unattended when the day's work was over. An open invitation to any passing thief.

There was absolutely nothing to be gained there so we took our leave of this ignorant sod and made our way back down Castle Street and High Street onto Saltmarket and turned left into St Andrews Street where the business premises I had to visit were both located.

The building was separated from the Glasgow District Court, also known somewhat tongue in cheek as *'The Palais de Justice'* by a narrow lane.

The lane was normally secured at the end of each day by means of a large metal gate which was about eight feet in height and had sharp metal spikes on top.

I couldn't imagine anyone scaling the gate and gaining access to the rear of the building very easily.

There was no other way to reach the back of the building.

I was assuming that the dirty deeds had been perpetrated from the relative safety of the rear of the property. I'd forgotten everything the old D/I, *'wee Bobby'* had taught me.

First and foremost was *'never assume anything son'*.

He once asked me: *"If I gave you a hundred pounds Willie, what would you do with it? A good detective has only one answer!"*

He tormented me for a couple of days before telling me: "Count it, never assume anything."

Both premises had actually been entered through windows at the front, bare faced cheek.

We called into the lawyer's office first, I needed a laugh.

The lawyer was there along with a couple of his staff, they were tidying the place up as the Scenes of Crimes officer had been and gone.

I made a mental note to give him a call later, he'd taken fingerprint impressions from the staff and they would be used for elimination purposes.

Any other prints found in the office could then be compared with those of known criminals in that area.

Criminals in a lawyer's office! Perish the very thought of it.

I could though maybe suggest a few names of likely candidates.

The office sported a quite new and modern looking alarm system on the wall next to the front door.

All flashing lights and a keypad.

I asked why the alarm had failed to sound when the window was smashed, the window being covered by the security device.

Strangely, for a lawyer, he told me the truth and admitted to forgetting to set the alarm when he'd left his office the previous Friday.

This poor guy who had only recently set up in business for himself knew his insurance company would without doubt renege on paying out and he'd have to foot the bill for the loss of a typewriter, a couple of phones and some small items of office equipment plus the damage to his property from his own pocket.

Life just gets better.

I must be getting soft in my old age; I forgot to inform his insurer about the alarm not being set. Must have had a lot on my mind that day!

There is perhaps a heart beating inside my manly chest after all!

Our next port of call was the adjacent leather warehouse.

We were met inside by two males who looked to be of Middle Eastern origin, perhaps Turkish or something similar.

Not best pleased doesn't begin to describe their mood.

"Have you got my jackets back yet?" was the greeting from the older looking man.

That wasn't exactly what was going through my head at the time

I was actually thinking about calling into a café on Gallowgate near to Glasgow Cross for a bacon roll and a cup of coffee.

Louise, the owner, makes simply the best Latte in Glasgow and there was at least half of a deep fried pig squeezed between the sliced Morton's bread roll which also dripped with real butter. Cholesterol, eat your heart out or just fur my arteries a wee bit.

Catching housebreakers at that time on a Monday morning wasn't high on my agenda. Breakfast was!

Housebreakers! All in good time.

I asked the impatient 'Turk' if there was any reason he could think of for his alarm not to operate when the window broke.

"What alarm?" was the reply.

An assumption on my part again!

I was a wee bit taken aback, a warehouse full of leather jackets and it wasn't even alarmed.

It occurred to me he wouldn't have been insured either, what insurance company would consider covering a business premises containing valuable items in that particular area of Glasgow and it didn't even have an alarm system installed.

Not as much as a fake alarm box on the wall outside.

Still, my job was to detect the person or people responsible, not to give advice on crime prevention to a man who had knowingly left his property unprotected.

Joe and I took little time inside the leather shop as there was nothing there of interest for us. Although, come to think of it, my wife Margaret would like a new jacket. I was brought up in the 'East' tradition after all.

Sergeant John McKenzie, you were the master blagger. I admired the way he filled his black bin-bag at the Barrowland market every week-end. What an expert.

Perhaps, just maybe, these Turks could receive the best of attention from Strathclyde's finest. Who? Me of course.

A good breakfast was called for, but Louise's place would have to do meantime.

No offence meant, I loved her Italian mum and dad, Rosa and Louis, the original occupiers of that wee haven at Glasgow Cross.

I never went short of a hot meal or a cup of tea when I was the 'beatman' thanks to them. Louise keeps up that tradition, I still, to this day, visit her café and have a coffee or tea with her.

Nostalgia is a thing of the past, so I'll continue with my inane ravings.

Dick Barton, the owner/manager of Dirty Dick's at Glasgow Cross next door to the infamous Mecca Bar was already seated at his usual place near to the front window drinking coffee when we entered the Criterion café.

Dick and I were not the best of friends, when I was a young 'rookie' cop working my beat at the bottom end of London Road and the Gallowgate many years before, I'd done the unthinkable and locked him up on the strength of a warrant which had recently been issued at the Glasgow District Court.

Dick had neglected to pay a fine for some trivial matter and a magistrate at the Palais de Justice in St Andrews Street had decided that a custodial sentence was now appropriate.

Barton never forgave me for doing my duty. Jailing him was a real pleasure which would also have annoyed some of the older cops who patrolled that beat on the other shifts. Their beer supply would be interrupted for a while. I didn't lose any sleep because of it.

I did however pee into his Volvo estate car's petrol tank when I'd had a few free beers in the Mecca bar next door, courtesy of the manager Leo Francetti. (book 1)

The car didn't turn a wheel for quite some time.

'Barton baiting' was now called for.

Dick would more than likely know who'd been responsible for *'tanning'* the leather warehouse. He could hear the grass growing in that low-life part of the city, nothing very much got passed him.

A decent turn like that would be openly discussed by the natives in his *'gang hut'*, the pool hall known as Dirty Dick's.

Getting him to tell me was the difficult bit.

He was studiously ignoring me, pretending to read his Daily Record newspaper, (his lips moved as he read) as I sat down opposite him at his *'windae seat'*.

Joe sat at another seat across the aisle from us.

Dick was hemmed in. It looked something akin to a Mafia hit.

Louise, the café owner, quickly disappeared into the back shop.

I wished him a good morning which was met with a grunt in response.

That was a start, better than nothing I suppose.

Polite conversation wasn't on the agenda that morning so I removed his newspaper from the table-top and crumpled it into a ball before dropping it to the floor.

It's so rude to continue to read when a superior being is speaking to a dung beetle.

No witnesses to the deed so no complaint could be made to my boss who wouldn't believe I could do such a thing anyway.

Dick raised his head and stared at me for a few seconds before uttering his words of wisdom.

"Ah f**ing hate you!"

Ditto Dick.

Now that the ground rules were clear, I asked if he would do a trade with me.

One piece of information from him to be met with another from me.

Quite simply, his car had been immobilised by some person putting a noxious liquid into the fuel system.

I would tell him the identity of that person in return for him telling me the true identity of the felons who'd *'screwed'* the leather shop.

Instead of being told to *"f**k off!"* as I fully expected, my old adversary looked at me and asked if I really did know who had disabled his Volvo Estate car and would tell him who had dared to do this foul deed.

"Aye, of course I know" was my reply.

He sat looking at me for a couple of minutes then said: *"Fat Andy and his pal Hector frae Airdrie look very smart in their new jaikets."*

Thanks Dick, that made sense.

There was a team of housebreakers operating from the Calton, The team were centred on a large family group which had a few outside acolytes amongst them. Andy and Hector were two of those hangers-on.

In a previous story I related a tale regarding one of that self same team who had assaulted a youth from the Calton by stabbing him through the face with a wooden fence post.

Two of the assailants who escaped prosecution on that occasion because of an eye-witness failing to speak up were none other than Fat Andy and Hector.

What goes around comes around as they say.

I thanked Dirty Dick for his assistance and rose to leave: *"who pissed in my petrol tank?"* asked Dick.

"Me," I replied and hurried from the premises along with Joe who was almost sprinting away along Gallowgate towards the Cross.

Not being an athlete, I just walked off quickly whilst frequently looking back over my shoulder.

Dick was known to be a loonie, capable of doing almost anything.

A knife from Louise's kitchen sticking in my ribs wasn't out of the question.

He had even been jailed once for attempting to burn down the High Court building in Saltmarket simply because his wife had been sentenced to a term of imprisonment for committing perjury during a trial there.

Taking revenge on an errant pisser wasn't implausible in his case.

I wouldn't be parking a car anywhere near to Glasgow Cross for a long time.

Fat Andy and Hector would now have to be seen and Joe's scaffolding enquiry still had to be dealt with.

Encountering Dick in the Criterion Café had resulted in us missing out on breakfast, we'd now have to go elsewhere and perhaps even have to pay for it.

A call in to the Grumbling Bum cafe in Bain Street was called for, we could thereafter adjourn to the police office to dine and have a well earned cup of brownish coloured liquid laughingly referred to as coffee.

With precious little else to occupy my mind other than solving the Glasgow Herald Wee Stinker crossword I sat at my desk whilst Joe being a lot more conscientious and diligent than I ever could be on a Monday morning checked his in-box for recent correspondence.

He let out a whoop of delight, his scaffolding had been spotted in a scaffolders yard somewhere near Falkirk by a builder who recognised the bright blue paintwork as being the marking used by the Dennistoun company.

Joe was then informed by the rightful owners as to the location of the stolen property.

A wee trip to Central Scotland Police area was now on the agenda for that day. A phrase book would also come in handy to help us converse with the locals and remember to end every sentence with 'Ae'.

Following directions to the yard supplied by the Dennistoun company I drove our 'state of the art' Maestro out of Glasgow, along the A80 trunk road to Castlecary where we took the road towards the outskirts of Falkirk and our destination, a scaffolding suppliers yard.

The double gates which afforded access to the premises by large vehicles were lying wide open when we arrived there unannounced.

As you might reasonably expect, there were piles of scaffolding poles and the paraphernalia that goes with them stacked neatly all around the yard.

There was even a minion happily painting out the blue markings on some of them

I think the sudden appearance of two men in Ralph Slater suits gave the game away; he rose quickly to his feet and scampered off to a portakabin

at the far end of the yard.

As we strolled over towards the cabin, a scrawny male of about 40 years emerged from the doorway.

Obviously the *'heid-bummer'*, he was wearing a tie.

Stating the obvious, Joe told him who we were and went on to tell the unhappy little man why we were there.

Asked about his possession of the pile of blue painted poles and their accompanying pieces, the man thought for a moment before telling us he'd bought them from a team of Irish tinkers whom he'd never seen before.

Maybe he did, maybe he didn't. But his problem now was that he had them in his yard and they were without doubt the stolen property Joe was looking for.

Joe perpetuated the story about them being Crown property and a hefty penalty could now be expected.

I wanted to tell the man it was actually a hanging offence to steal from the Crown but you can take it too far, a good public flogging would have to suffice.

Joe phoned the true owners and spoke with the managing director of the company. A suitably impressed and satisfied customer.

Some-one from that company would still have to identify the recovered scaffolding as being their property before it could be returned to them.

That was done within the hour and later on in the day the *'buyer'* from Falkirk loaded it all onto one of his own flat-bed lorries and transported the lot back to the Cathedral precincts. How the lorry driver knew to return the scaffolding without being told where it'd been stolen from was quite remarkable. Joe and I just let it go, there was little point in pursuing the matter any further.

We also attended at the handover just to ensure there were no fisticuffs between the rightful owner and the tinker from Falkirk who claimed now to be out of pocket. Nae luck!

Joe later reported a case to the Fiscal's Office but that was the last we heard of it. I don't know if the Fiscal even proceeded with a prosecution.

Joe's blood pressure could return to something approaching normal now and I could hunt down Fat Andy and his mate Hector.

There was still the matter of the missing leather jackets to resolve, not forgetting the housebreaking at the lawyers office.

I suppose even lawyers can be sinned against.

Finding Fat Andy was never going to be a problem even though he was homeless and moved from one crony's hovel to another frequently.

During the daylight hours he would often be found sitting on the doorstep of his *'gangleaders'* end of terrace house in the Calton.

I don't believe this cretin was ever allowed inside and was kept at the door by the *'lady'* of the house, the leader's mother.

Hector lived in Airdrie and for some unknown reason had teamed up with this mob from Calton in Glasgow.

I can only guess where this liaison began, where? I wonder would criminals from different parts of this country meet up with each other.

Let me think!

He would be more difficult to pin down than the fatter half of the duo.

Enough for one day, we could go hunting for bad guys the next day unless something more pressing happened before then.

Being the East, that was never out of the equation.

Tuesday dawned and I was a bit more alive, Mondays don't suit me very much. I think Monday should be abolished and replaced by making Sunday last for 48 hours.

No point in going out looking for Andy much before 11a.m. he would require his beauty sleep and was rarely seen before then.

If you're out prowling about for half of the night looking for something to steal or somewhere to break into then I suppose you're entitled to a long lie the following morning.

I would take Joe for a run in the car to give him time to sober up, let his bloodshot eyes settle down and generally kill some time.

It would probably be that damned Maestro again as I was never in the office early enough to seize the keys to a decent car. I believe some other officers were awake all night to ensure they didn't oversleep and be landed with that dog of a vehicle.

It's little wonder that the British car industry failed when they produced rubbish like that.

We drank our coffee, emptied the paperwork from our correspondence *'dookits'* and fled from the office before the grumpy D/I appeared from his room across the corridor and noticed that Joe was still a bit under the weather and smelled like a brewery.

This particular D/I didn't approve of drink and come to think of it I don't believe he approved of very many things which gave people any pleasure.

I don't know if he had any children or if there were there must have been a lodger living in his house.

The thought of him... No, it doesn't even bear thinking about.

It's disgusting!

Joe and I drove down to a certain café at Glasgow Cross for more coffee and a scan through our correspondence.

He opened a brown coloured envelope from within his pile of accumulated bumph and read the letter contained within.

"We've to call in at the scaffolding place in Dennistoun today Wullie, they want to see us."

"There's probably a bottle in this for us."

Trust him to think of that, I was thinking more of a box of chocolates. My arse! A sealed container would do nicely thank you.

Fat Andy was back on my radar now, coffee and a huge bacon roll, the half pig version, had steadied my neighbour. We were ready to roll again.

A tour around the Calton and the area surrounding Glasgow Cross was now required. Fat Andy and his cronies never ventured very far from there. They were thieves and robbers, this was their hunting ground.

It would also be mine.

Our safari took us round about Gallowgate, Moir Street, London Road, Glasgow Cross, back along Gallowgate up to Bain Street where we stopped outside Betty's fish shop. A freshly made cup of tea could always be had in her back-shop. A big tin kettle which must then have been about fifty years old would be boiling away on a gas ring.

Almost immediately a young female member of the clan we were looking for appeared on foot from the pedestrian area at the end of Claythorn Street, right in front of us.

She was resplendent in her new cream coloured leather jacket.

The girl displayed a shocking lack of dress sense though, she was carrying a bright blue coloured handbag which clashed with the jacket. Even I know that cream and blue don't go together.

We'd have to detain her in our guise of the fashion police.

'Less than amused' doesn't begin to describe her attitude when asked to assist us with our enquiries.

She was the younger sister of one of the main players in the faction we were interested in and she was wearing a brand new leather jacket.

Into the back of the car with her!

"Nice jacket pet, where did you get it?"

Stony silence, not a word.

She'd been well schooled, Calton born and bred, there was no way she'd *'burst'* to anything.

A trip to the police office was called for; I told her that I suspected her to be in possession of stolen property, *i.e. the jacket.*

Still silence.

With her safely out of the way in a detention room, we made our way down to the leather warehouse in St Andrews Street in possession of the young lady's jacket.

The older Turk was there and immediately identified the jacket as being from his stock.

He described the label inside without being shown it and said that style wasn't even on sale yet. The batch containing that particular type of jacket had only just arrived in the country so no-one could possibly own one.

Superb, that would do for me.

Little miss huffy could make her mind up now, she could be charged with the initial crime of theft by housebreaking at the warehouse along with a charge of reset of one leather jacket or on the other hand she could tell me who did the *'turn'* and where could I recover some or all of the property. Good cop, bad cop my backside. This was a case of bad cop and really horrible cop. She knew what to expect from us as one of her brothers had done a bit of time because of Joe and I. That desperado had stuck a fence post through an innocent young guys face a couple of years before this incident and we'd jailed him. She'd be wary of us.

I would of course threaten to have her kept in a cell for an appearance at Glasgow Sheriff Court the following day.

There wasn't a hope in hell the duty officer would agree to keep her in custody for being in possession of one stolen jacket but she wasn't to know that was she?

I opened the door to the detention room, Eva, the German born female turnkey by my side. I believe her maiden name was Brown or Braun or something similar.

The Caltonian female suddenly sat bolt upright on the wooden bench seat.

It may just have had something to do with Eva pulling on a yellow coloured rubber glove.

Eva liked to have her little joke!

She had two sons in the police. They were in the Stasi, the secret police in East Germany.

I lie, Dougie worked in the Glasgow City Centre Division and the other one, Bob worked with me in my beloved East.

Both are decent human beings.

One stern look from me and the imperious figure of Eva standing alongside was too much for wee huffy, she burst into tears, time to go for the jugular.

Do you want out today or what?

"Aye, Mr Greenshields sir!"

That was much better, now for the real business of the day.

Who did the turn at the leather place and where are the jackets now?

The little bitch sat on the wooden bench and stared at the floor for a couple of minutes without uttering a sound then asked if she was really getting out.

"Yes, when I've got the jackets,"

"John and fat Andy done it, some o' the jaikets are in oor loft, the rest o' them are away. They've been selt. Don't tell them ah telt ye, John'll f**king kill me".

John is her brother; he's the animal who Joe and I'd jailed a few years earlier for stabbing a young man through the face with a fence post. Fat Andy was simply one of his acolytes.

Locking them up for a theft by housebreaking would give me enormous pleasure. I detested them. Vermin who lived by thieving and had never worked a single day in their miserable lives.

Leaving the now sobbing female in the care of Eva I sought out the duty officer, a uniformed Inspector and told him of the developments.

A very obliging chap, he agreed to hold onto the female whilst I made hasty arrangements for obtaining a warrant to search the *'gang hut'* in Calton occupied by John and his tribe.

To think that Strathclyde Police were actually paying me to inflict grief on these scumbags still warms the vacuum in my body where normal people have a heart.

The warrant application pro-forma was quickly filled out and checked for errors or omissions before Joe and I headed off to the Palais de Justice aka the Glasgow District Court in St Andrews Street where we would seek out a Magistrate to grant our request and authorise the search.

No problems were anticipated and none were encountered, we had the relevant piece of paper and could now go out to play.

A *'posse'* was gathered from the local plain clothes unit who were only too happy to oblige when asked to assist in searching this nest of vipers.

The front door to the end of terrace house usually lay open with fat Andy seated on the doorstep like an overweight garden gnome.

This time he wasn't there but the door was open, the way in was clear.

Two plainers at the back door, Joe, a plainer and myself in through the front door and one plainer to stay with the cars.

John was seated on a couch in the livingroom whilst his father and mother were in the kitchen. They were all less than pleased to see the police in their hovel and some of the words used to greet us would make a sailor blush. None of the sisters were present; they were probably patrolling the Glasgow Green near to the Peoples Palace earning a couple of pounds from the men who circled the area in their cars looking for a *'girl'*. It was simply how these females made their money. A nice family.

John actually rose from his throne and faced up to the first cop as he entered the room, it's not as though he didn't recognise who we were.

He's just a vicious, aggressive, horrible individual.

It was a bad move on his part as the cop, normally a quiet big lad, pushed the cretin on the chest sending him staggering back and landing on his backside on the floor.

The *'godfather'* of this crime family, a *'Fagin'* lookalike, had emerged from the kitchen obviously intent on doing battle but when he saw who he was about to deal with any thoughts of offering up some violence very quickly disappeared from his head.

He and his wretched son would've lost the argument and I'd have had the satisfaction of meting out some much deserved police brutality, purely in self defence you understand.

All three were gathered together in the livingroom and shown the warrant which gave us the power to search the house and to open any lockfast places we may encounter.

Fagin wasn't a happy man when told that we were looking for stolen property, leather jackets to be exact. He shot a glance at his son as if to say: *"this is your fault."*

I asked them if there were indeed any leather jackets in the house and was met by silence.

That response was what I'd anticipated anyway. Not a family who were disposed to helping the police with their enquiries.

They weren't however, denying there were leather jackets somewhere in the house. We'd have to find them for ourselves.

Not being entirely stupid and going straight to the loft, thus giving the game away that we already knew where they were stashed , we made a show of thoroughly searching the entire house starting from the ground floor and working our way steadily up through the three upstairs bedrooms and the bathroom. The maid perhaps had the day off as shit stained underwear and socks rigid with dirt had congregated on the floor below the unmade beds and the toilet pan contained an unspeakable mess. She would have to be spoken to for neglecting her duties.

The bed linen was just a tad off-white too. This was a job for Rentokil.

Nothing had so far been found, nothing I'd want to touch that is.

Just the loft to search now and it was padlocked, to keep thieves out no doubt.

John, who had been present whilst the search was being carried out, was asked to produce the key to unlock it.

"Huvnae goat ane" was the not unexpected response.

English Translation: *"Sorry, I don't possess such a thing officer."*

Not to worry, there was a large key in the form of a crowbar in the car-boot. That'd do nicely.

John pointed to a piece of carpet on the landing floor outside the door to the stinking toilet and said: *"under there".*

Joe stood on a chair and unlocked the loft hatch; John looked decidedly uncomfortable now and was shifting his feet. I got the impression he was about to do a runner. The big plainer obviously though that too and took hold of the little weasel by the arm. If he tried to make off, the big guy'd rip his arm off. I'd have enjoyed seeing that happen.

As the hatch door opened we all got a waft of the aroma given off by new leather.

I smiled at John, he didn't reciprocate. How rude, he'd no manners!

Joe hauled himself up into the loft-space, switched on an electric light, a bare bulb which dangled from the rafters and shouted down to us that there was a pile of leather jackets lying on the floor of the loft.

I looked at John whose face showed clearly what was going through his mind.

We'd found the stolen property in his father's loft and John had given us the key to unlock it.

"Wee man, you're getting the jail and so is your Da, it's his house and the gear's in his loft".

I love it when a plan comes together.

A good recovery of stolen property and I also get to send one of the most despicable people I've ever come across to the Sheriff Court charged with committing a theft by housebreaking.

Joe called down again, *"Wullie, there's a new looking typewriter and a couple of phones underneath the jackets".*

It doesn't get much better than that.

I would've asked John about incident at the lawyer's office when interviewing him on tape later on but now I really had something substantial to put to him.

The lawyer would without doubt identify the office equipment as belonging to him.

This was a good day; it was all falling very nicely into place.

We would have the office stuff carefully preserved for fingerprint examination and a pound to a penny there would be some very interesting impressions found on them.

Even if I failed to obtain convictions for the initial crimes of theft by housebreaking, I would at least get them done for the crime of Reset which carries the same penalty as for the original offence. Either way, I win!

John now did something totally out of character for him, I was utterly astounded.

"Leave ma da oot ah this, ah'll take the derry."

English Translation: *"Leave my father out of this, I'll take the blame."*

Asked if he'd admit to how and when he'd perpetrated these two crimes and describe on tape the interior of both crime scenes so there could be no doubt that he'd been there. Totally crestfallen, he replied, *"Aye".*

Who was along with you?

"Naw, ah'm no sayin that".

You've got to ask, haven't you? I'd just have to wait for the result of the fingerprint examination.

I had a result, that's what really mattered.

The grumpy old D/I would be off my back for a wee while at least.

The female, his sister, was released from her detention before we arrived back at the police office, it wouldn't be very clever of us to let them see each other.

She'd without any shadow of a doubt become the victim of his anger when he did finally get out.

Then again, maybe he should have just a peek. No, No, No, even I couldn't stoop that low. Or could I?

There may even be a detention form lying on the charge bar with her details on it!

My nickname was merited and I had reputation to uphold after all.

The lawyer got his property back after it had been examined. For some reason or another, I don't know why, I never did get a result from the fingerprints people. These things happen I suppose. No system's perfect.

Just glad it wasn't a murder.

I called in to see the Turk to return his property, to my surprise I was greeted with a smile and offered a huge discount by him on any jacket purchased from him. Another satisfied customer.

Joe and I had another task to complete before we finished work for the day.

The scaffolding company in Dennistoun had still to be visited.

There was the small matter of a glass container to be dealt with.

On our arrival at the premises we were ushered into the owners office, he was seated behind a very plush looking desk and got to his feet to greet us, offering us his hand.

We had a few 'large halfs' with him and left with our prize after about an hour.

It wasn't wrapped in glass but my wife Margaret was soon to be the owner of a new jacket made from the softest brown leather...

DRUGS SQUAD 3

Don't drink the wine

There is a story in the bible whereby Jesus performed a miracle at a wedding ceremony by turning water into wine, I know someone who could also do that trick but he did it in the reverse order. The wine became water, or perhaps even a bit of a mixture.

A detective sergeant at the Drugs Squad when I was there had received information regarding a man who lived in a posh block of flats on Great Western Road near to Cleveden Road in what I believe is the Hyndland area of Glasgow.

The male was alleged to be dealing in Cocaine from this rather upper class and select building which even had its own uniformed caretaker who was based in a small office located at the front entrance.

It had been reported by several of the residents that the man in question was receiving callers at all hours of the day and night.

The callers used the intercom system which was also located at the front entrance to the building to contact him and he in turn would allow them access.

His visitors rarely stayed for any great length of time before exiting again.

I don't know why the informant thought it was Cocaine that was being dealt in this instance, perhaps it was because this was an upper class area and toffs don't use Heroin or Amphetamine to the same extent as the lower orders do.

The detective sergeant made some enquiries into this person's identity and background only to discover that he was an unemployed barman with a criminal record which contained a string of convictions for petty thefts and minor assaults which were mostly perpetrated on females.

Apparently he was only about 5 feet 6 inches in height but was known to be violent. I often wonder if it is a Glasgow or West of Scotland trait where little men try to be *'big men'* and are more prone to show aggression and violence to others than their bigger brothers do.

Anyway, the detective sergeant decided he'd enough evidence of drugs dealing in douce Hyndland and duly sought and obtained a warrant to search the dwelling for controlled substances.

I actually thought the information was a bit sketchy but it wasn't my problem, I was, as always, only too happy to go along for the ride. Besides my name wasn't on the warrant request and I didn't have to justify it.

I may be a bit cynical in my old age but the mere fact an ex-Chief Constable of the City of Glasgow Police resided in the same block of flats as the *'bad man'* may have prompted the sergeant's decision to go ahead with the search.

Yes, I probably am being an old cynic! Things like that just don't happen. Do they?

About six o'clock on a Friday evening five of us piled into a couple of the nondescript Drugs Squad *'hit cars'* and made our way from police H.Q. in Pitt Street, Glasgow to the leafy suburb of Hyndland.

I felt as though I should have been in possession of my passport, I was as out of place there as a Jew would be in Palestine.

I'm a boy from Shettleston, the worst and most deprived area in Glasgow. I wasn't brought up in a street with trees in it.

There had once been a row of trees in Stamford Street in the Barrowfield not far from Shettleston. As I recall, the natives who had recently been resettled there from the badlands north of Alexandra Parade had found a use for the beautiful Beeches and Elms. They chopped the trees down and burned them in their once all electric fireplaces.

Sorry, back to the real plot...

The caretaker had been alerted to our presence and admitted us to the building which even had a carpeted entrance hallway.

So different from my usual haunts, the tenement closes of my beloved *'East'* which smelled like the public toilets at Bridgeton Cross.

I thought all closes smelled of urine until one day, long before I'd become *'a druggie'*. I strayed into the *'South'* on another matter and actually saw a woman washing the stairs in her close.

I wished I'd had a camera with me; the other detectives in the East would accuse me of lying or being on the booze if I told them what I'd just witnessed.

The lift door opened and in we went, the sergeant looked at me and said: "nae gratuitous violence." The other three just smirked. If only I'd known what *'gratuitous'* meant.

Up we went, the doors opened and there just to the right of where we stood was the flat occupied by 'Mr Big'.

Even the hallway leading from the lift to his flat was carpeted which was an unexpected bonus for us, we could approach his door very quietly.

It was a black coloured heavy wooden door with three Ingersoll locks, one near the top, one in the centre and one near the bottom of the door.

I gave the door a wee push at the top and to my surprise it gave way a little, the top lock wasn't set. I did the same with the bottom lock, it too was unlocked.

C.D, the poor sod I nearly killed on his motor bike (in book 2) very gingerly turned the door handle and opened the door. It hadn't even been locked.

It was a cavalry charge now; the livingroom was directly opposite the front door, I could see into that room as the door to it was lying open.

I ran in and found it to be empty; the others had run down the hallway which was off to our right shouting that they were the police.

The posse was met near to the kitchen door by an Arthur Askey lookalike who was all for fighting with the police.

He disappeared under the weight of four bodies and still tried to box with them.

I stood at the livingroom door and watched the fray, the phrase 'nae gratuitous violence' crossed my mind but I thought better of it. The sergeant could be a vindictive little sod too at times and would certainly attempt to find me a rotten job to do later on.

Whilst they were still scrapping with the poison dwarf on the hall floor, I retreated into the livingroom. Just to the right of the door there was a dark coloured sideboard, mahogany I think and very old fashioned. Something out of the 1920s or 30s.

The dwarf had a set of five decanters sitting on top of the piece of furniture each about half full with what I took to be red wine and white wine.

The sound of battle had died away after a couple of minutes so I looked out into the hallway to offer my assistance to the others. The sergeant's reply was unprintable. The angry bantamweight had been 'subdued' and was now sitting on his hall floor looking as though he had just gone two rounds with Mike Tyson. He was pulp.

Gratuitous violence? Never!

It was only a one bedroomed flat so searching it didn't present us with any great problems. The fighting bantam of course denied having any Coke in the flat but after about 10 minutes or so of diligent searching we found it concealed under loose leaf tea inside a caddie in the kitchen.

There were about 20-25 paper wraps each containing £20 worth of the white powder.

He could argue his case in court, no doubt his defence would be the usual *'the drugs squad put it there'*. Same old... Same old...

As we were leaving with our prisoner I couldn't help but notice that the decanters were now almost full and one police officer was smiling.

Miracles do happen occasionally you know. Water into wine etc.

Whilst in police custody the now accused suddenly became homeless, the caretaker, on the instructions of the property owners, had changed the locks on his door and our victim was evicted for failure to pay his rent, maintenance charges and for anti-social behaviour. There may have been more to this raid than I was ever privy too.

I wonder if the dwarf ever got to drink his wine or did the caretaker perhaps?

They say: *"What you don't know won't hurt you."* I'm not so sure about that now.

Deals on wheels

It has long been known in police circles that an awful lot of taxi drivers are fully aware of the fact some of their *'fares'* are on their way to buy controlled drugs.

"Wait there driver, I'll be right back!" will be familiar words to many of them.

How many times does it take before a driver realises he or she has taken fare paying passengers to the same address and a similar ritual is gone through.

They aren't stupid, all they are doing is turning a very blind eye so as not to lose any business, a junkie's money is as good as anyone else. Or is it?

Cab drivers bleat loudly enough when one of their number is assaulted and robbed and aren't then slow to seek police assistance.

Consider how many drivers have been robbed and injured, even murdered whilst going about their lawful business and the offender is none other than last weeks fare paying junkie.

Whose money had he been using to pay for the ride?

I'm not suggesting there is no come and go between individual police officers and some taxi drivers, I of course can attest to the situations whereby ongoing crimes have been reported by passing taxi drivers and the perpetrator has been arrested thereby saving time and taxpayers money on any resultant criminal investigation.

My friend *'Tam the taxi'* (Book 1) was a classic example of a driver keeping the police (me) informed of suspected dealers addresses which came to his notice as he drove about the streets of the City of Glasgow.

He was instrumental in causing the demise of a good few drugs dealers and a number of major players through his own diligence and attention.

Tam was a class act.

However, there are also some drivers who are more involved in the dealing side than just knowing or suspecting what is really going on between a fare and a man living in a frequently visited close in Scotstoun , Maryhill, Possil or dare I say it even my home town East Kilbride.

My often harassed and tormented Detective Sergeant W.McK. now happily retired and immune from me, stuck his head round the door to the Drugs Squad general office early one Wednesday evening just to see who was available.

He'd received a call from a *'friend'* to say a taxi driver in East Kilbride was selling deals of Cannabis Resin from his taxi whilst he was working for a company based in the town.

I was told by *'my leader'* that people were phoning the taxi company and requesting this driver in particular be sent to collect them. There were also rumours circulating around the employees of the company that if anyone wished a bit of *'blaw'*, Michael was the man to see.

He was either a very good driver of course or maybe a bit cheaper than some others or perhaps there was a darker reason. We opted for *'darker'*.

This sergeant was a real worker and had already done his homework before telling me the story.

Michael was on shift at that time and would be driving about the East Kilbride area probably into the early hours of the next day.

His next shift would commence at 5pm on Thursday.

He lived alone in a one bed-roomed flat in a tower block known as Old Vic Court in the Calderwood area of the town.

It was decided we would go out to E.K. and have a look at the flat to ascertain the possibility of doing the deed there or if that wasn't a viable option we could always have him stopped in the street by a marked police vehicle if there was one available. Their availability was never guaranteed for any number of reasons. Tea breaks and a long queue in the chip shop being the most common. Call me an old cynic or am I simply being realistic?

The block of flats in question is the centre one of three fourteen storey buildings named Globe Court, Old Vic Court and Sadler's Wells Court.

Old Vic Court was the one we were interested in, I won't mention which floor he lived on, suffice to say it was on an upper level.

Although there was a secure entry system in operation at the front and rear doors all we had to do was wait until someone exited from the front door and we walked in.

It really makes a nonsense of the term *'secure entry system'*. There was no-one to monitor the comings and goings from the buildings.

Taking the lift to the appropriate floor we emerged from it and turned right along a very short hallway, there was a window on the wall facing us, I looked from the window and could see into Michael's livingroom. There was no sign of life, so far so good.

The view from that landing window was outstanding, we could see clear across the Clyde Valley, taking in most of the city of Glasgow to the Campsie Hills and far beyond.

A view, in my opinion, wasted on a dung beetle of a drugs dealer.

We examined the door to his flat; it was quite insubstantial, constructed of wood and had one Yale type lock. There was a spy-hole at eye level but that in itself wasn't a great hindrance. We could get around that little problem.

The hallway was about 10 or 12 feet in length from his door to the fire-escape door, if force was required to open his door then I'm sure the sergeant would be only too pleased to take a run from the farthest part of the hall and head-butt it open. His head being the thickest part of his body. (He would of course take a run-up and put his boot to the door just above or below the lock.)

The plan was simple and straightforward, just as well, because I was simple and the sergeant was the other bit.

We knew when he was due to be back at work the next day, so the sergeant decided we would come back about an hour before he was due to go on shift and just knock on the door.

I would obtain the search warrant before I'd even reported for work.

A local J.P. now sadly deceased, a great friend to me and my colleagues duly did the needful and we were ready to roll.

This time we took 'silo arse' with us, if we put her up to the door he would without doubt look through his peephole first and see a female on the landing. He probably wouldn't suspect anything was amiss, just so long as she wasn't asked any hard questions such as: "Who are you? What do you want?"

'Silo' wasn't good at ad-libbing but she was tall and blonde.

It was a bit cold in the car as we drove the eight or so miles from Glasgow to East Kilbride with the windows open but having experienced her gas emissions before, the sergeant and I decided to brave the chill wind. She could have bottled that stuff and sold it as nerve gas.

Aromatherapy it wasn't.

Tony Blair could have found his W.M.D. there without having had to invade Iraq.

Again, it was so easy getting into the building, a nice old lady even held the door open for us as we approached from the car park.

Into the lift I went along with the sergeant and *'silo'*. We were in the horrors, having had experience of her in a lift before. The stink is almost indescribable; a crime against humanity is about as close as I could get to it without swearing.

We got out of the lift on the floor above Michael's flat, thankfully without incident and came down the fire-escape stairs to avoid passing by his living-room window.

I'll give *'Silo'* her due, she went straight up to the door and rattled on the letter-box.

The Sgt and I were pressed hard up against the wall, I'll re-phrase that, we were hiding out of sight.

Much to our surprise and utter delight, the clown opened the door, we rushed forward, pushed *'silo'* out of the way and barged into the flat.

For all he was a big lad, there was no resistance offered by Michael.

He didn't even ask who we were.

I still recalled the other sergeant's edict of *'nae gratuitous violence'*, it was never gratuitous but if it was asked for or even demanded, it was delivered without hesitation.

After the preliminaries were gone through in the hallway, the sergeant and I took the now detained Michael along his short and rather dingy hallway into his equally dingy living room. There, on top of a coffee table was an L.P. record cover, (the Beatles White Album to be exact) and sitting on the cover was a lump of resin which weighed about 6 ounces, twenty four cut pieces all weighing about an eighth of an ounce each, a set of brass scales complete with weights and a sharp knife which had a carved wooden handle in the shape of a fish and a brown stained blade.

The only thing missing was the clingfilm to wrap it in but as he was still in the process of cutting the *'Dope'* to size, the wrapping could come later.

When asked to account for his possession of the substance, scales and knife, he smiled and said: *"It's just a bit of personal."*

This one would go to trial, nothing was surer.

Willie McK. reported the case to the Fiscal's Office at Hamilton and we carried on with business as usual, nature would take its course. If there was indeed to be a trial it could be six to nine months further on down the line.

Given the circumstances of our finding a lump of *'dope'*, ready made deals, scales and a stained knife I would've thought he may have done the decent thing and put his hands up. It was a nice clean capture.

Not so.

Willie and I were cited to appear at Hamilton Sheriff Court for the trial.

I never liked having to attend at Hamilton Sheriff Court at any time as there were no separate waiting rooms for police, witnesses, accused persons and their defence witnesses.

We all had to wait in one room until called into court to give evidence.

It simply wasn't right.

Listening to 'the neds' talking amongst themselves could actually be quite funny. If the words *"what's happening man?"* and *"Ah went and he went, so ah pure went and he pure went man,"* were taken out of the English language many of these cretins would be totally unable to speak.

Please don't ask what the last *'ned-speak'* sentence means, it beats me.

Our trial began just before eleven o'clock in the morning, it was a working day so just to make matters worse we weren't even earning a bit of overtime.

Willie was called in first and emerged after about thirty minutes, he wasn't allowed to speak to me after giving his evidence in the courtroom of course, just in case we colluded and I would change my evidence to coincide with his... As if?

He winked and gave me a wee smile as we passed in the corridor outside the court-room.

The Usher led me into the court and showed me into the witness box before announcing to the Sheriff who I was.

The accused was sitting a few feet away from me, off to my left.

He was seated with his back to the Sheriff and was grinning from ear to ear, if I'd been in his position I think I may have had slightly different emotions. I'd have been filling my breeks.

The Depute Fiscal who is the Crown prosecutor, led me through my evidence and had me explain to the court why the accused had been charged with the more serious offence of possessing a controlled drug with intent to supply it to another rather than possession for his own use.

I knew he would have asked my *'neighbour'* Willie the same question and I also knew he'd get the same answer from me.

Simple, if it was for his own use, why bother to sub-divide it into smaller weights. All he would require to do was wrap the large lump of dope in clingfilm to stop it from drying out and cut a piece from it when he wanted to roll a joint.

Going through the process of weighing and cutting the deals was both unnecessary and pointless if the cannabis was really only *'a bit of personal'*.

The Fiscal was clearly satisfied with my explanation and sat down.

The defence agent rose to his feet, he looked for all the world to be about fourteen or fifteen years of age. I think when the accused took his case to a lawyers office the senior partner on listening to the tale had decided this was a no hoper and should be allocated to the *'boy'*, the trainee who ranked just above the office junior or tea-lady.

This poor sod hadn't a clue about drugs and didn't know the right questions to ask. He must have gone through university with his head inside a brown paper bag.

The Sheriff obviously felt sorry for the *'boy'* as he himself asked me about values, weights and the reason for there being no wrapping material found at the time. The lawyer should have asked these questions and didn't.

I looked over to the taxi driver as his defence agent sat down somewhat sheepishly.

The smile had now gone from Michael's face.

His Lordship, the Sheriff had opened a paper folder which lay in front of him and was reading through it quite intently so I took my opportunity and gave the accused a large smile and a wink.

The absolute hatred showing on his face was a joy to behold. I simply love it when you know you've got to the bad boy and hit a raw nerve.

The Fiscal saw what I'd done and buried his face in his hands, his shoulders were heaving as he tried very hard not to laugh out loud.

When he looked up again a few minutes later I could see the tears of laughter streaming down his face which he was wiping with a handkerchief.

I may not have been receiving an overtime payment for this one but the entertainment value itself was priceless.

I was excused from the court and glanced over to the Fiscal as I left, I swear to God he was shaking his head and there were still tears running down his cheeks.

Willie had waited for me in the W.R.V.S. tearoom which is located on the ground floor at the front of the building. He was nursing an empty tea-cup and no doubt waiting for me to appear and buy him a fresh cup of his favourite drink along with a chocolate biscuit. Chancer!

We went over the questions asked at the trial and reprised our answers.

You would have thought it had been rehearsed, we were almost word perfect.

Rehearsed? Never! And the accused is now an ex-taxi driver.

Who's smiling now Michael?

A return to Port Glasgow

G iven the choice, I'd without doubt never have set foot in this black hole in the universe again but being a serving police officer there was no option but to do as I was instructed.

Some-one in the upper echelons of the police had decreed there was a body to be had in conjunction with multi kilos of Cannabis resin being couriered weekly by train from London, the final destination being that blot on the landscape known as Port Glasgow.

The only other time I'd had the misfortune to visit the place was when a waxed jacket I'd lent to another Drugs Squad officer out of the goodness of my heart was returned to me bearing the tell-tale skid marks of dog dirt down the front of the now unwearable garment.

Along with another six Squad members, the only ones on duty and available at that time because of court commitments, I was despatched to Motherwell railway station with the aim of reaching it before the Glasgow bound express train from London Euston did.

Apparently this train was carrying a courier who was believed to be in possession of a large holdall bag containing twenty or so kilos of cannabis resin.

Just one wee problem, we didn't have anyone on the train following his every movement nor did we know what he looked like.

A needle in a bloody haystack if ever there was one.

I was teamed up with John (vile) Kyle who was to drive our vehicle and 'A', a decent enough guy who made little impression on me or the job in general.

John Kyle most certainly did.

The train was due at Motherwell within thirty minutes and we were in the centre of Glasgow.

I anticipated what the immediate future was to bring and wished for a change of underwear.

John would pilot the car from police headquarters in Pitt Street onto the East bound M8 motorway at the Charing Cross on ramp and head towards Motherwell.

I was in the front passenger seat and sat with my eyes closed and hands clamped to the sides of the seat as he wove at speed through the increasingly busy afternoon traffic. 'A' was quite understandably cowering in the rear of the car and had gone white at the gills. Well, as white as he could ever be given his ethnic background.

A couple of times I ventured to open my eyes and glance over in John's direction. He was smiling and every now and again the swine looked at me and laughed.

Even when he pulled off the motorway and drove into the one-way system at Motherwell he hardly took his foot off the accelerator pedal until we reached a small car-park in front of the railway station.

I thanked him from the heart of my bottom for the experience and got out of his chariot happy to still be in one piece.

The London train was due in less than two minutes; He had achieved the almost impossible without bending the car although he'd probably shortened my life span by a few years.

We now had to find our man, providing he got off the train there at all.

It wasn't unknown or even uncommon for couriers to get off the train a stop or two early as a precaution, the police would normally expect them to stay on until the last stop, Glasgow Central or perhaps alight at Motherwell.

We made our way to a gallery which overlooked the single platform where the express would halt before continuing on to Glasgow.

I saw a man standing on the Glasgow bound platform, I recognised this fellow from an encounter we'd had years before.

He was a television pundit and frequent guest at the Police College at Tulliallan Castle in Fife where he schooled young detectives in the art of giving televised interviews.

My abiding memory was of him being ushered into a classroom where I was seated along with about thirty other budding young sleuths.

He was wearing a cream coloured suit which bore a huge wet piss stain below the crotch on the left leg.

I couldn't take him seriously after that, every time I saw this 'celebrity' on the T.V. I pictured the big pee stain on his trousers.

The train duly appeared and a few people disembarked from it. No-one, to my mind anyway, fitted the profile of the suspect drugs courier.

Instructions were now received from our leader at Pitt Street, we were to make all speed and get to Glasgow Central Station before the train arrived there.

Here we go again and the motorway traffic would be much heavier now.

John Kyle was smiling at me again. My heart sank into my boots. Would I ever see my wife again? Aye, every cloud has a silver lining!

As we hurried back to our car my attention was drawn to a white coloured Rover 416 hatchback parked in front of the station. I'd seen it parked there with its engine running when we'd first arrived.

The female driver had alighted from her vehicle and was eyeing us very intently.

She was about 40-45 years of age, small and slim, very smartly dressed in a jacket and matching skirt and had distinctive long auburn hair which looked as though she spent money in keeping it well coiffeured.

From the back she really looked to be quite attractive, shame about the face.

She resembled a ten year old shrew that'd just drunk a bottle of vinegar.

Once seen, not to be forgotten.

I took a mental note of the Registration plate and jotted it down on a scrap of paper as I got into my co-pilots position beside the *'Kamikaze'* Kyle.

I had a bad feeling about that Rover car, something wasn't right.

The express train had already left Motherwell so we were now playing catch-up.

I really did close my eyes as John again weaved in and out of the rush-hour traffic drawing quite a few curses and stony stares from other road users on the west bound M8 and city streets as we sped towards Glasgow Central Station, this surely had to be a forlorn hope.

I honestly don't know how he did it but as we skidded to a halt at a Royal Mail bay in the station the London train was beginning to spill its human cargo onto platform 2.

It obviously takes a bit of time for the passengers to file off so we were on hand to view the majority as they emerged through the gate and onto the main station concourse.

We still didn't know who were looking for, it was simply a case now of winging it, playing it by ear.

The suspect would have been a male of about eighteen to twenty years of age, probably travelling alone and would more than likely only have one large holdall bag in his possession. Isn't the profiling of criminals just wonderful? My arse.

About half an hour or so had come and gone, the stream of passengers had by now dried up. John and I were almost the only folk still at or near to platform 1.

We'd waited to the very end in case our man had also waited and would emerge when there were few people around.

Personally, if I was him I'd have tried to mingle with the crowd, the odds of making a clean getaway would obviously been much better that way, but who knows, we had to wait anyway.

The *'stand down'* was called and feeling a bit deflated after the excitement of the high speed antics on the road we turned to head for the car which was lying abandoned, still angled across the Royal Mail bay.

Then I saw her, the shrew featured woman from Motherwell Railway Station, she was loitering near to the Gordon Street exit from the station.

This pedestrian only exit is the nearest one to platforms 1 and 2 where the London train arrives and departs from.

I had that intuitive feeling in my water; she just had to be the *'clue'*.

The woman apparently hadn't noticed us so we made our way into a bar which overlooks that part of the main concourse and watched her from inside whilst also having a beer.

We had to blend in with our surroundings you understand.

The job could be tedious at times.

She hung about for about fifteen minutes, obviously waiting or looking for another person but met up with no-one in that time and eventually turned and left the station.

We followed on foot a good bit behind and weren't too surprised to see her enter a multi-storey car park in Dundas Street where she went straight to her white coloured Rover hatchback which was parked on the ground floor.

Time to call it a day, no point in giving the lady any idea that we had probably now found a bit of a clue as to who she was and perhaps she may even lead us to the elusive courier.

That evening before I went off duty, I ran a check on the car Registration number.

Surprise surprise, the vehicle was registered to a female who lived in Port Glasgow.

We now had an address to covertly visit the following day if the boss was still interested in finding the message boy.

I checked with the Electoral Register to ascertain who lived at that address, no surprise to discover that only three people were recorded as staying there.

Two males and a female.

The older male and the female weren't on file, neither had any previous convictions and no intelligence was held relative to them.

The younger male, obviously the son of the house as he had the same Christian name as the other male was a quite different kettle of fish. In Glasgow parlance, he was a *'ned'*.

A thief and a convicted drugs user with recorded links to other more serious players in the area. In the great scheme of things this young man was the ideal candidate to be our courier. A *'gopher'*.

Next morning, bright and early, having had the go-ahead from our esteemed leader, K, a nice man, a very nice man, John, *'A'* and I took a covert vehicle, a totally nondescript grey coloured Renault 19 and took off westwards along the M8 motorway.

John was again doing the driving, but this time thankfully obeying the speed limit and driving on the right side of the road.

There was no hurry now; we had all day to play with.

The address we had to find was, according to our map, somewhere on the outskirts of the town.

Picking our way through the run-down streets which were lined by equally run-down housing and wound uphill from the main road to Greenock and beyond, through what was very obviously bandit country towards the address to which the car had been registered, I was already beginning to think this was a *'bridge too far'*.

Anyone who wasn't known to be local was going to stick out like a sore thumb.

To make the situation even worse, the house we were looking for was located in a cul-de-sac and could only be approached from the front as there were only fields to the rear.

This venture was rapidly going down the tubes.

Driving into the dead end street wasn't an option, time to ad-lib.

John stopped the car outside a wee shop about a quarter of a mile away from the subject address and I set off on foot back towards the house.

It was located immediately on the right at the entrance to the cul-de-sac and was the first house in a row of four similar terraced dwellings with common closes between them. The windows, both upstairs and down, were fitted with venetian blinds and all were in the closed position.

I cannot be one hundred percent sure but I thought I saw an upstairs blind twitch as I was having a look at the house.

Time to make an exit, but without making it too obvious. Was some-one watching me? I still believe so.

There were also three blocks of flats in the street, one directly opposite the address we were interested in with a further two blocks at the bottom of the road. Seeing there were no vacant flats in the first block I walked on downhill to the other two buildings.

The sound of a car engine suddenly came from behind me, I didn't want to look and carried on walking, making my way into the nearest block of flats.

Once inside the building I turned and peered through the dirty glass panelled doorway. It was the wee Rover I'd seen in Motherwell and Glasgow and the same female I'd seen before was making her way from the roadway to the house.

She opened the front door and entered, the door couldn't have been locked.

From my vantage point I could see there was no pathway or road at the rear of the terraced houses, simply fields and hawthorn hedges.

The rear garden of the subject address was separated from the garden of a house in the adjoining street by just such a hedge; it must have been about six feet in height. I couldn't be sure but from where I was standing there appeared to be a gap in the hedge separating the two gardens. There was no way I could get any closer to obtain a better view without being seen myself; I'd have to let it go.

There didn't appear to be any *'empties'* in these blocks either.

Not wanting to hang about in case anybody appeared from one of the flats I made my way up the street, past the house and back to the car where John and *'A'* were waiting.

John wasn't happy; the natives had been paying a bit of attention to the *'squad'* car as it obviously wasn't known in the area. We couldn't use it in that part of the town again.

They weren't stupid; the car had been noticed and was now a matter of suspicion and interest for them.

It could have belonged to the police or even worse, *'the Social'*.

As we sped along the M8 motorway towards Glasgow I related to John and *'A'* what I'd seen.

There was no place to watch the suspect address from and any type of mobile surveillance was out of the question.

What to do?

I spoke with the boss on my return to Pitt Street telling him about the lie of the land, he was of the opinion we couldn't spend much more time on this job as there was something else more pressing in the offing.

Ideally I'd like to have *'put it on the back burner'* and had another look at the job again later but there are only so many times you can do that before there is a back-log which is too big to deal with and the jobs are *'binned'* anyway.

The only other realistic alternative was to *'hit and hope'*.

Not ideal but rather that than let it go without even trying.

An *'executive decision'* was made by *'K'* the boss: *"Just hit it!"*

The necessary paperwork was obtained and about 9a.m. the following morning, six of us in two *'hit cars'* sped off along the M8 motorway towards the Greenock, Port Glasgow and the west. I exaggerate when I say *'sped'*. We actually crawled along through the rush hour traffic which didn't clear until we actually exited from the motorway at that hole in the universe which is Port Glasgow.

There was no point in hanging about, there wasn't any place to take observations from so it was simply a matter of coming to a halt a short distance away from the address to be searched and thereafter making our way there quickly on foot.

The word *'quickly'* doesn't in fact apply to me, the others would be in the house and having their tea by the time I arrived. Fleet of foot, I am not.

The front door to the house was closed and locked as was the door to the common close which gave access to the back garden. With no access to the rear, we couldn't secure the property.

It was all going wrong.

After about five minutes of banging and shouting, the front door was opened by the shrew woman in her nightgown who it has to be said is even uglier in the morning than later in the day when she is wearing her warpaint. Her hair was like something akin to a crows nest on a bad day and her skin required a coat of plaster never mind rouge or powder.

She was shown the warrant, allowed to read it herself and said she was quite happy to have the house searched for controlled drugs.

I made my way upstairs with a couple of the team and on making our way into a front bedroom we discovered the *'ned'* lying in his bed. He didn't seem at all phased at our appearance and was smirking. I had a bad feeling about this.

The duvet cover was pulled back to reveal him wearing socks and pants in bed.

His trousers, shoes and shirt were lying in a heap on the floor; I picked the shirt up and felt warmth from the material. The bastard had been wearing it shortly before and had stripped his clothes off probably as we arrived.

Suffice to say, nothing of value to us was recovered there, we'd lost.

It isn't nice but it happens.

We went through the motions of searching the upper floor of the house but knowing full well the resin was gone.

The words of wisdom from a previous sergeant *'nae gratuitous violence'* were running through my head.

Have you ever had an urge to take the smile off someone's face?

I growled and his smirk quickly disappeared. The cautioning words of my old sergeant had saved this reprobate from summary justice... This time.

I had a very short fuse.

Making our way back downstairs, I came face to face with Mrs Shrew features standing in her hallway.

She looked startled at first, my boyish good looks no doubt, then said, *"Motherwell, the station, you were there"*.

No point in denying it, she'd recognised me.

I gave the woman my best attempt at a smile and exited from the house leaving the sergeant to *'give her the yellow card'*.

Losing like that really sticks in my craw, even now years later it hurts.

A week or so after that debacle, *'K'* stopped me in the corridor outside his office.

He told me what had actually occurred that day in Port Glasgow.

We'd been seen in the street by the wee ned's sister, we had left our cars parked outside her house which backed onto the one we would be searching.

She suspected what we were about and alerted her mother and brother to our presence and imminent arrival, the cannabis was quickly transferred from one house to the other via the gap in the hedge.

A lack of forethought on our part, we didn't even know there was a sister nor that she lived almost next door. A salutary lesson had been learned, do your homework properly in future.

I never saw the wee ned or his ugly mother again, probably just as well.

I have been known to hold a grudge and my cautionary sergeant had now retired.

Friendly fire in Stevenston

As much as I really don't want admit to this incident, I feel I'm duty bound to relate the story because it actually happened and the whole point of this trilogy of books is to *'tell it like it was'*.

We read and hear reports of victims of friendly fire practically every day. The newspapers, T.V. and Radio news bulletins are forever telling us that our American allies and quite often our own troops have fired upon and killed or injured members of their own side.

Well, to a much lesser extent I did it too, not in far off Afghanistan or Iraq but in a much more lawless and dangerous place than those previously mentioned, this incident occurred in an Ayrshire coast town known as Stevenston.

Neither Basra nor Helmand Province can hold a candle to this place.

I would put it on a par with Barrowfield in my beloved East End of Glasgow where the natives eat their own weans.

Our Det/Insp Eddie McColm was himself an Ayrshireman born and bred,(I also have Ayrshire blood in my veins, my mother Sadie was a Dux Medallist at her school in Girvan) had received information regarding a family in the town who were selling Cannabis Resin in large enough quantities to merit the Strathclyde Police Drugs Squad showing an interest in them.

Eddie did the necessary background checks and being satisfied with the veracity of the information and the good intentions of the person supplying it, he decided to go ahead with the operation.

Taking observations on the house to be searched was out of the question, it was located too deeply into bandit country, there would be no friendly faces here if we were to be discovered.

We would have to send out a scouting party to have a quick look just to familiarise ourselves with the area and to, if possible, try to ascertain a way to approach the house without being seen.

I was delegated along with R. B. to go out for a look-see.

We set out for Stevenston about 6 o'clock on a Wednesday in one of the Squads covert surveillance vehicles, it was so nondescript it was almost invisible to the human eye. Just tickety boo.

Finding Stevenston was the easy part of the job, all we had to do was follow the road signs for Irvine then turn off the main road and head for the huge I.C.I. (Nobel) plant which dominates the skyline there.

The dwellings surrounding the factory were bog-standard 1940-1950 council built houses. Some were terraced; some tenement type flats and others were four in a block maisonettes

This was a depressing hole of a place, I believe it was built to accommodate the Glasgow overspill. These were simply Glaswegians transplanted into Ayrshire to work in the Nobel factory.

You can take a horse to water, but you can't make it drink. Some of the offspring of the original people who'd moved here hadn't worked a day in their lives and probably never would.

The house we wanted to look at was occupied by first generation 'Stevenstonians', they were quite simply Glaswegian neds who were born somewhere else, which just happened to be outside the City boundaries.

It was located top right in a four in a block. Entry was gained by means of an open doorway on the ground level which gave access to a flight of stairs which in turn led up to the front door of the subject flat.

Not easy but definitely not impossible.

On reporting back to the Det/Insp, Eddie, at Pitt Street with our findings, he made what I considered to be the correct decision.

Am I a pretentious bastard or what?

A test buy!

We would send some-one up to the house with the intention of making a purchase of drugs, then when we were sure there were drugs being sold from that address we would go through with the 'hit'.

Who would do the test purchase for us I wonder?

It had to be some-one who would be above suspicion.

Some-one the occupants would never suspect of being a police officer.

Someone who in their wildest dreams could never have been a police officer.

Unfortunately FiFi was unavailable, she was either on annual leave or doing yet another night school course learning about aromatherapy. A misnomer if ever there was one.

We would have to look elsewhere.

Amar would do the job for us.

This young man was as brave as a lion, he'd been with the Squad for about a year and cooked a delicious chicken curry twice a month for his colleagues.

What more could we look for in a Squad member besides a discount at his friends restaurant and an invite to his wedding?

He was approached by the D/I and I believe a few other members of the team with regard to his doing the test purchase.

There never was any doubt that Amar would volunteer for this quite risky task as he'd been used in this capacity before, but always in the city, never though in the outlying areas where at this time there were relatively few ethnics around.

He was expendable anyway...

I jest of course, Amar was a good guy and his curries would've been sorely missed.

The following Friday evening, again about 6 o'clock we set off from our base in Glasgow and headed off down the coast.

The team consisted of one D/I one D/S and six other assorted specimens of pond life of which I was one.

We set off in two *'hit cars'*, cars which were only to be used for direct action, never in any situation where surveillance would be employed.

These vehicles were normally big powerful beasts, capable of extremely high speeds and usually quite spacious to accommodate our equipment. (Equipment! that reminds me of a story regarding the naivety of a very senior officer)

Anyway, by the time we arrived in Stevenston it was quite dusky, light was fading and the street lighting was beginning to glow yellow prior to coming on full.

Eddie primed Amar and directed the poor sod to the house in question. He was to go to the door on his own and ask if he could buy a quarter ounce of Hash using the marked £10 notes he'd been supplied with

If successful, all he'd to do then was return to his vehicle and show the drugs to the supervisor in that car.

Dead easy!

Off he went, into the close and up the stairs to the door of the evil drugs barons flat.

We all sat quietly in the hit cars hoping all would go well with Amar, if anything went wrong we'd never be able to replace his curries as he didn't share the recipes with us.

A smart move on his part.

About five minutes later he re-appeared onto the street and walked away out of sight of the bad guys flat.

I watched as the other car slipped almost silently away to recover our hero. A few anxious minutes elapsed before the radio crackled into life. Amars' venture had been unsuccessful.

There was allegedly nothing for sale at that moment, but if he came back in about an hours time if he could have as much as he wanted

At least they didn't give him a hard time of it by asking how he knew to try to buy Hash from them.

It could all have gone very wrong if that had happened. Ad-libbing wasn't his strong point, brave as he was. Eddie asked Amar if he was up for it again, would he give it another go?

No hesitation, of course he would.

Instead of hanging around the place and sticking out like sore thumbs, the natives wouldn't have taken very long to suss us out, we drove down to Irvine to pass the time.

I was getting hungry but stopping for a fish supper wasn't really advisable, can you imagine having a square go with an angry man and you have just devoured a big bag of greasy fish and chips?

I could always have been sick on him I suppose!

I'd just have to suffer the hunger pangs a bit longer.

Here we go again, it's now about 8.30 p.m. and quite dark. The street lighting made very little difference and the close into which we were about to send Amar had no internal lighting at all.

Eddie again asked Amar if he still wanted to go through with this.

"*Aye*", was the immediate reply. Brave boy indeed.

Amar entered the close and mounted the stairs, we filed in very quietly behind him and listened as he asked for his Hash.

"Aye, nae bother mate, in ye come."

The door closed behind him.

Two or three minutes later he was back out and coming down the stairs, well maybe it was him, it was so dark I couldn't tell who was there. That's my story anyway.

As the figure approached me I grabbed him around the neck and gave him three rapid on the face with my right fist.

Oh shit! It was Amar.

He had the Hash clenched in his left hand and was now bleeding from both nose and mouth.

The others pushed past us and someone knocked on the door which was opened almost immediately by a startled female.

In they went, I heard a bit of shouting at first then it all went quiet, the good guys had prevailed and the house was secured.

I apologised to Amar and told him to act as though he also was now a detainee.

He mumbled something about me not being his friend now and I think he said the word *'Fatwah'* or it could have been *'fat bastard'*, I'm not sure.

He was hauled bodily into the flat where the occupants were all seated on a couch near the front window.

One of them, a tall skinny man with a Mohican haircut was less than amused when he saw the blood spattered face of poor Amar.

"Nae fuckin need for that, big man" was his retort.

Amar's true identity was safe now, we could use him again in that neck of the woods as he was now a hero. Unless of course we had to produce him in court as a witness, then he'd be a marked man.

Two kilos of hash was duly recovered along with the marked £10 notes and a case would be prepared for the attention of the Fiscal at Kilmarnock in due course.

Time to adjourn back to civilisation and perhaps even have a beer at the end of the shift.

Back at the office I again made my apologies to Amar,but he was having none of it. He wouldn't even look at me.

The D/I, Eddie and the D/S. Willie entered the general office with a sheaf of paperwork in their hands.

Amar got off his backside and left the room.

I was presented with everything from Racial Abuse complaint forms to allegations of racially incited assault on a colleague.

I was appalled until Amar stuck his head around the door with a huge grin on his face and said,

"Not so bloody smart now are you whitey?"

Note to Amar.

This is a little known fact, privvy only to Eddie, Willie McK and myself, it was actually Eddie and Willie who put me up to it. They said I should bloody you a little just to make it look good.

A Fatwah on them also?

Sorry, It wasn't just me my friend. Loved your wedding *'by the way'.*

A wee footnote regarding obligatory equipment

An enquiry was launched by Strathclyde Police's hierarchy into the alleged use by Drugs Squad officers of unauthorised equipment following a complaint by a convicted drugs dealer.

His dog had allegedly been pummelled by a police officer.

Some officers had reportedly been seen carrying pick-axe handles whilst engaged on otherwise quite lawful activities and some-one had perhaps laid into the bad guy's dog with one.

A very senior officer, a Chief Superintendent no less, who is known to me personally (he actually quite likes me, I think he's an ar**hole!) was appointed to investigate the allegation and this man took time to interview every member of the Drugs Squad individually within a Detective Superintendents room on the 4th floor at Police H.Q. in Pitt Street, Glasgow in an attempt to ascertain what the truth of the matter was and exactly what equipment was available to us.

The reason given for the possession and use of pick-axe handles was very straightforward.

They were used to ward off vicious dogs when houses were being searched for illegally held controlled substances.

Drugs dealers aren't known for keeping poodles, it wasn't uncommon to come across pit bull terriers and the like when going about our business.

These dogs aren't pets, they're kept because they are dangerous to humans therefore clouting them with a long, heavy piece of timber is to my mind quite acceptable.

Self preservation is the name of the game

I already have a long scar on my right forearm courtesy of a bad dog. I didn't want another one. Besides, I'm a handsome devil and a scar on my face would be totally unacceptable to me.

No more mister nice guy where dogs are concerned. Hit first, don't wait to be bitten.

The Chief Superintendents decision was to summarily ban with immediate effect the use of pick-axe handles on dogs.

It's all very well for him to pontificate regarding the striking of a dumb animal with a big stick. The dog wouldn't be biting his arse if he was safely ensconced in a warm, comfortable office drinking coffee, fawning over his personal typist and dreaming of his M.B.E or whatever.

His solution to the dangerous dogs' problem was brilliant in its simplicity, I suppose that's why he was a very senior policeman and I was no better than an amoeba, pond life.

The Drugs Squad were to take possession of a long wooden pole with a large V shaped construction at the business end. If you picture a bricklayer's hod in your mind then that is what it resembled, only a bit bigger.

There was also another long pole; this one had a noose at one end. The noose was intended to ensnare the angry dog. What we were supposed to do then with the animal certainly baffles me. Personally, I would have beaten it to death with a pick-axe handle but then again I didn't now have access to one. I would have to kill it with the 'brickie's hod'. Once a bastard, always a bastard.

The final touch to his master-plan was to have the Squad members carry riot shields when going out on a drugs raid. The shields could then be deployed as extra protection from dangerous dogs.

So we now have a supposedly covert unit of men and women trooping through the streets of Glasgow or wherever carrying an outsized 'brickie's hod', a lasso on the end of a stick and a couple of riot shields.

I think the drug dealers may just have smelled a rat and suspected the Drugs Squad were in town, either that or it may have been the seven dwarves on their way to work!

Heigh Ho, Heigh Ho, it's off to search we go.

We've got our tools and look like fools.

Heigh Ho, Heigh Ho, Heigh Ho, Heigh Ho...

This insanity was foisted onto us by a man whose claim to fame within the police service was that he'd never once given evidence in a court of law.

A real practical hands-on police officer if ever there was one... My backside.

His equipment is probably still gathering dust in the cupboard where it was abandoned, unused and unloved.

About as useful as he was.

I retained a pick-axe handle along with my unblemished, rather boyish good looks...

I wonder what this man's *'Lump sum'* and pension amounted to when he finally retired from the job?

A wee bit more lucrative than mine maybe? But I'm not bitter. Am I?

What goes around comes around

This all began when I was a young detective at London Road police office in the early nineteen eighties, I almost said the early nineteen hundreds but I'm not quite that old.

Joe C and I were partners, he'd not long returned from a long stint at the Drugs Squad and his head was still full of Drugs, Drugs, Drugs.

Everything he saw or touched was drugs related in some way.

I was still pretty naïve regarding that part of the job and wouldn't have known a controlled substance if I met it in my soup.

Joe had inherited an enquiry, something to do with the theft of materials from a building site and the chief suspect was a sixteen year old 'Barrowfielder' by the name of Heaney.

I knew this human dung-beetle from some previous dealings I'd had with him, he was being brought up in the faith and would be a thief like his father before him and his father before him and so on.

We made our way to the hovel occupied by this tribe in Mountainblue Street, Barrowfield. It was located ground flat left in the close.

As Joe and I approached the close-mouth, Joe looked in through the bedroom window; there seated on a single bed was the boy we wanted to speak with.

He was happily puffing away on a cannabis joint. A reefer.

We entered the close and knocked on the door. It was opened by the lady of the house who was sporting a large blackeye, a gift from her husband.

Joe asked if could come in and have a word with the boy and also pointed out to the woman that her son was smoking dope in his bedroom.

I don't think she was playing with a full deck and just stepped back out of the way to let us enter the flat.

Making our way into the front bedroom, we found the boy. He was less than pleased to see us and threw his joint down the back of his bed whilst trying to conceal another one under his pillow.

Not exactly the crime of the century.

We confiscated the cannabis.

I think all Joe was intending was to tell the boy off regarding the cannabis and question him about the theft allegation.

All hell broke loose with the dope-head screaming, shouting and running around the room like headless chicken.

The mother came rushing into the bedroom to find out what was happening to her little boy. Were the big bad policemen beating him up? Not this time, he was still only a tiddler.

She was told to bring him to the police office later, when he'd calmed down. He could be spoken to there.

Joe and I returned to the office for the obligatory cup of coffee and perhaps even a few frames of snooker in the games room.

About an hour had passed when we received a call from the front desk; a man was at the office asking to speak to us.

Reluctantly putting down our snooker cues, we made our way downstairs to the C.I.D. general office.

There, sitting at the public reception area outside the C.I.D. room was Heaney senior. He'd a ratlike face and oozed evil, you could almost taste it. He personified badness.

As I made my way towards him he suddenly burst into a fit of rage, shouting and swearing at Joe and me.

What did we fucking think we were doing bursting into his fucking flat and planting fucking drugs on his son!

I wouldn't have done very well as a career diplomat.

Heaney's face was pressed up against mine and I could smell his vile breath.

Enough was enough.

I really should simply have locked him up for a Breach of the Peace in a police office but instead he was gripped by the scruff of the neck and marched to the front door and heaved out onto the street.

How I restrained myself from booting his backside I'll never know. The urge was almost overwhelming.

A *'complaint against the police' i.e. me*, was now absolutely guaranteed.

The cretin wouldn't miss such a golden opportunity as this to cause me a bit of bother.

Not daring to return to London Road police office, he took himself along to Shettleston where he made his complaint to the duty officer.

The following day I was summoned to the Detective Superintendent's Office and asked to account for my actions.

I related the story just as it had occurred, no fibs and no deviations from the truth. That was the difficult bit for me, but as I saw it, Heaney had got off lightly.

The boss sat behind his desk and gave me a long hard look before asking: *"Why didn't you just boot his arse Wullie?"*

'Get out, Ah'll deal with it'.

Joe was sitting at his desk which faced mine; he was in the horrors regarding this *'horrendous complaint'* as he saw it.

I had on my sad, worried face as I trudged across the floor. Joe asked how the interview had gone, I replied I'd been told to clear my desk and the boss wanted to see him immediately.

The colour drained from his normally florid complexion and he rose to his feet whilst reaching for his lounge suit jacket which was draped across the back of his chair.

"Joe?" I asked: *"Are you selling that suit, you'll no be needin it again?'"*

I gave him my best *'you've just been done'* smile and offered to buy him a much needed shot of caffeine.

Something a wee bit stronger was called for, Joe liked his bevy but it was far too early in the day, for me anyway.

I wasn't flavour of the month with Joe for a few days but he came around and just hated me now rather than loathing the very sight of me.

Heaney never came near me after that incident; I could very easily have been tempted to sink my size nine brogue into his scrawny arse. I believe he may just have realised that.

A few years later when I was a Drugs Squad officer working from Police Headquarters in Pitt Street, Glasgow, my old buddy from the early days of Tobago Street and London Road, Detective Sergeant Keith Macdonald approached me and asked if I recalled a *'Barrowfielder'* by the name of Heaney.

I actually had to think about it for a few seconds then the penny dropped. Yes, I remembered that weasel.

They say that what goes around comes around.

Keith had information from one of his touts to the effect that Heaney who now had another wife had moved away from the Barrowfield and was dealing heavily in Cannabis Resin from his new home in Leithland Road in Pollok.

Keith asked if I'd go there with him for a look at the house and we could perhaps identify any vehicle or vehicles Heaney had access to.

Haud me back !

A chance to pay Mr Heaney a visit, polish up the size nines. Here I come.

We took one of the covert cars and drove across the city to the Pollok district; it was at that time a bit on the rough side and could've been twinned with Beirut or Gaza City.

Although I don't believe either place would wish to be associated with Pollok as it may have got them a bad name.

Leithland Road was a bit of a hole, marginally better than the Barrowfield but then so was Gaza and it had to be patrolled by U.N. Peacekeepers.

Heaney's house was located on the left as we travelled downhill away from the police office and fire station. It was a three apartment terraced house set in a row of five similar dwellings. I noticed that the curtains hanging at the front window and the two upstairs bedrooms looked to be filthy. The front garden was overgrown and littered with all manner of debris. Obviously not a fan of Gardeners World.

There was a blue coloured Renault 9 parked on the street outside the front 'garden' gate.

A quick check with the control room staff back at Force Headquarters revealed the vehicle to be registered a Mr T Heaney at that address.

If Keith's information was as normal, absolutely correct, then we had a 'goer'.

The first part of the story was spot on, Heaney was living there, given that was confirmed, then why shouldn't the rest of the information be correct also?

He'd been told by the tout that our man was delivering quantities of cannabis resin to customers throughout the city on an almost daily basis using a motor vehicle.

With any luck at all we had now identified that vehicle.

Covert surveillance on Heaney was now called for.

Keith laid the intelligence package before the Detective Superintendent, a nice man, a very nice man and after little or no persuasion the go-ahead was given, we would take Mr Heaney on.

Surveillance within a housing scheme is difficult, fraught with danger and has many pitfalls. The first one being the natives, they aren't all stupid and an unfamiliar car parked up for even a short period of time with one or two people on board can and probably would raise suspicions amongst the inhabitants that all wasn't well.

Direct observation in this case was out of the question.

I won't go into great detail about how it was achieved in this case but suffice to say when the subject of the operation attempted to leave the housing scheme we would be with him very shortly.

The first day of interminable watching and waiting came and went, there were no sightings of Heaney and the car remained parked outside his house all day, not turning a wheel.

A fact confirmed by the occasional drive-by of Squad vehicles at different intervals of time.

We had been on him since about ten o'clock in the morning and time was wearing on, Keith called the stand-down just after 9pm.

At the debrief back at headquarters we all agreed to stay with it until ordered not to by the bosses, Keith wasn't often wrong and I had a feeling in my water, this one would come good.

Another day dawned with the same troops and same cars but we'd each take a different location to sit and wait from the previous day.

The same car in the same location two or more days in a row isn't good thinking.

Again we were in place about ten o'clock in the morning, his vehicle was still parked outside the house. Apparently in exactly the same position we'd left it in the night before.

Maybe he wasn't even in the house!

Nothing for it but to wait patiently, one crew member observing whilst the other read or closed his/her eyes.

Time dragged by again, the papers were read and puzzles completed, (well, in my case). Subjects to talk about dried up.

Silence in the car, I never liked to have a radio station playing whilst on a watching job; it could be so easy to miss a call on the police radio because of music playing or whatever.

4.30 pm. As if out of the blue, there he was right in front of me; he'd emerged in his Renault from Leithland Road onto Crosstobs Road where he performed a right turn onto Brockburn Road.

My neighbour in the car was broadcasting the speed and direction of our quarry over the police radio within seconds of our spotting him.

One by one the others in the convoy responded to our call and were falling in behind us as we tailed him at a safe distance.

He was taking us on an odyssey as he visited various addresses throughout the city of Glasgow, houses and flats in Pollok, Corkerhill, Mosspark, Craigton, and Cardonald where he joined up with Berryknowes Road, onto Moss Road and thereafter through the Clyde Tunnel picking up the A814 Clydeside Expressway towards the city centre. Heaney wasn't employing any anti-surveillance tactics and didn't even look in his rear view mirror very often. We could have followed him in fleet of New York Yellow Cabs and he wouldn't have noticed or presence behind him.

I was beginning to think we'd perhaps left it too late to take him out, an awful lot of stops had been made and his stock must be depleted when Keith came on the radio.

He, in my opinion, quite correctly called the stand-down.

We'd seen more than enough that day to establish what Mr Heaney was all about.

Heaney was dead meat.

The debrief back at the office was very simple, nothing much to complain or fight about.

The deed would be done the next time he moved in his car, the same tactics could be employed except this time we'd strike at the first opportunity.

The following day was a Thursday; we could reasonably expect our man to be a bit on the busy side now.

Thursdays onward until Sunday were our busiest times with recreational drugs, cannabis at that time being the most prevalent.

Off we go again to our respective positions; there is a feeling of genuine optimism about the team. I wanted so much to be in at the *'kill'*.

A wee bit later in the day, this time about 5.15 pm. he was spotted by another member of the squad. Same route out of his street as before, we fell in behind and waited for our chance.

This time he headed off directly to Rutherglen where he made a brief stop at a tenement block in Greenhill Road which connects Mill Street and Stonelaw Road, two main roads which dissect Rutherglen.

Keith decided to let him run a bit yet.

I wished he hadn't, but the big fellow was the boss and it was his operation after all. I was still only cannon fodder.

Off we went again, no stops this time, right across the city to Kelvingrove. Keeping tabs on the subject through city traffic is a bloody nightmare at the best of times but during the peak hour when the traffic is nose to tail it is so easy to become stuck and the bad guy simply disappears out of sight.

He was actually lost twice during the operation but thankfully was quickly re-sighted each time and the *'follow'* continued.

As we travelled along University Avenue near to Glasgow University it occurred to me he would probably have customers amongst the student population there.

His car slowed and came to a halt on that leafy boulevard and Keith called the hit.

One car stopped in front of him, another as close as possible to his rear so that he couldn't manoeuvre and make off. A third then blocked his exit from the driver's door.

We all piled out of the squad vehicles, the third car reversed away giving us access to the driver, my old mate Heaney.

The passage of time hadn't mellowed him one little bit, the tirade of obscenities issuing from his vile mouth was only what I'd expected.

He'd managed to lock the car doors in an effort to keep us at bay.

His window and the front passenger window were summarily smashed by two big boys who hailed from Ayrshire. Must have been something in the school milk, these men were huge. I was dwarfed by them.

Heaney had now drawn a knife which had been concealed in the driver's side door pouch.

As he lifted his right arm to present his knife at the two giants, they pulled him out into the street through the broken window whilst still wearing his seat belt.

The weapon was quickly dropped when he realised this wasn't going to be his day.

Needless to say the car contained a good haul of neatly packaged quarter ounce deals of Cannabis Resin ready for onward sale and a roll of bank-notes.

He would also be charged with possession of an offensive weapon and assaulting two police officers by presenting a knife at them.

I hadn't played any great part in this incident so stood back whilst the arresting officers took charge of Mr Heaney and placed him in the rear of a police vehicle.

Heaney saw me as I stood talking to Keith outside the car; the look of recognition on his face was instantaneous.

I just smiled, winked at him then walked away. He again blew up and I could hear him ranting and raving that I'd *"f**king set him up."*

Revenge is very, very sweet indeed. Thank-you, Keith.

Heaney was taken to the nearby Partick Police office to be processed where for some unknown reason he was seen to be holding his arse as he walked across the car-park straddled by his two large Ayrshire bears.

I'd worn my shiny size nine brogues that day especially for him.

Academy Street

Icould best be described as being a refugee from the *'East'*. I began my police career in that Division and never forgot my roots even after being away from the area for quite some time.

There were of course occasions when I'd return there on Drugs Squad business and having a good working knowledge of the place and its inhabitants helped.

One of the D/I's at the squad had information regarding a male who was alleged to be selling heroin from a flat in Academy Street which is in the Shettleston area of Glasgow and is policed by my old *'E'* Division.

I knew the area very well having been born in nearby Kenmore Street and living for a time in Wellshot Road before escaping to East Kilbride along with my parents, brother and sisters.

Academy Street is located as its name suggests beside what used to be Shettleston Academy just off Shettleston Road near to its junction with Old Shettleston Road. My grandfather, George Greenshields worked in the academy kitchens in the late 1950s.

The D/I told me that he'd arrested the male a few years earlier for having committed an unprovoked serious assault on a man in Glasgow City centre and that he was well known for his acts of wanton violence.(He missed his vocation and should've joined the Drugs Squad)

His record of violence stretched back for years, beginning when he was still attending primary school. A real nutter.

I thought it strange I'd not heard his name before but it transpired he'd come from Pollok originally and had only recently migrated eastwards, something do with him being re-housed away from Pollok for his own safety.

The D/I kept tabs on him and had been informed by *'an interested party'* of what he was now doing and where he was doing it from.

I volunteered to give it a look, not being totally altruistic I must admit. There may have been a bit of overtime to be had during the operation and perhaps a citation for court later on which could also generate some loot. Especially if the court appearance fell on my day off.

Mercenary doesn't even begin to describe it.

Street dealers are ten-a-penny but when things are quiet with the bigger targets then why not turn the screw on the bit part players instead. Pressure on the minions could sometimes provide an insight into how their suppliers were going about their business.

Then again it could be a complete waste of time and the street dealer wont speak up. You've got to try though haven't you?

The flat occupied by the subject was located on the first floor of the building, it consisted of a living-room, kitchen, bedroom and a bathroom. I used to live in an identical tenement flat when I was a wee boy.

The living-room window overlooked the street, the bedroom and kitchen were to the rear and looked out onto the back courts I played in as a child in the mid 1950s.

The door to the close was a bit of a problem as it had a secure entry system in place and it unfortunately was in good working order.

That could be taken care of later if our observations pointed to dealing taking place there.

A couple of days were set aside to allow for surveillance to be employed.

Shettleston Road is a very busy thoroughfare, the pavement would be filled all day with pedestrians going about their lawful and for some, not so lawful business.

Hanging about the street, watching the comings and goings from a close was a non-starter. The natives would soon enough smell a rat.

Plan B. now applied.

Enquiries were made with the council Housing Department who obliged with a set of keys for an empty flat on Shettleston Road which afforded us a reasonable view of the close and living-room window.

This wasn't going to be anything special and not a lot of manpower would be required to establish exactly what was happening in Academy Street.

I was in the empty flat from 9a.m until 9p.m. each day for three days, Tuesday, Wednesday and Thursday.

Twelve hours overtime and not a ball kicked yet.

It was like spearing fish in a barrel.

The custom wasn't the busiest I've seen but it was there all the same. I obtained a few photographs of the building to show to the troops before they set off after the Friday afternoon briefing at headquarters. It helps when you know which close to enter.

A fairly steady procession of gaunt junkie faces to and from the close, mostly arriving on foot.

The East end of Glasgow, Shettleston in particular, is recognised as being one of the most deprived areas in Scotland, if not Britain.

Junkies don't have money to waste by spending it on taxis very often, money buys smack.

All used the door intercom system before being admitted

Some even appeared at the living-room window to have a look up and down the street. Very obliging of them, that confirmed which flat was being visited.

I suspected they were looking out in case the police were about.

Well, they were right we were there and we were watching them watching out for us.

I'd noticed the same two people, a male and a female arrive at the close on each day I was there. He was about five feet ten inches in height, very thin and slightly stooped. The girl could only have been about five feet tall and equally as thin as her male companion.

What set them apart from the other callers was the fact that they always stayed a good bit longer than the rest before leaving.

The D/I was kept informed of the progress by means of an encrypted radio set (cannot be scanned) and the 'turn' was planned for early Friday evening, a search warrant was already in place having been obtained from Glasgow Sheriff Court whilst I was engaged elsewhere.

One thing still had to be attended to, the controlled entry system at the door to the close! It would have to be disabled before the turn was executed.

The Housing Department people were very helpful but couldn't supply me with a spare key for the door, needs must, I would have to deal with this little problem first thing on Friday morning whilst the door was open to allow the postman and milkman etc access to the building.

About eight o'clock on Friday morning the close was visited by a somewhat ageing vandal who emptied a tube of superglue into the door locking mechanism whilst it was in the unlocked position.

It was highly unlikely to be repaired before the following week at least.

The way was now open for the Drugs Squad to come calling in the early evening.

It was probably going to be a long day for me.

So long as nothing else of any real importance cropped up between eight o'clock in the morning and seven in the evening this job would be put to bed as planned.

I had to attend Glasgow Sheriff Court as there was a drugs trial I was involved in scheduled for that day. I could concentrate on the present and put the evenings' operation out of my mind for the time being. It wasn't a big deal this trial, but allegations of impropriety had been made by the accused and as per usual the defence agent was basing his case on *'the Drugs Squad planted it'*

Staying out of jail myself was the priority now. I cannot imagine spending even one night in Barlinnie Prison.

A hated C.I.D./Drugs Squad officer locked up alongside my previous customers, no thanks. Living on Mars Bars and praying never to drop the soap in the communal showers wasn't my ideal.

I absolutely detest criminal defence agents.

The word *'criminal'* in my opinion sums them up.

It has been said that prostitution is the worlds oldest profession closely followed by lawyers. Not very much separates them in reality.

Prostitutes make money by pandering to needs, Lawyers make their money by pandering to neds. Neither have much in the way of morals. It's a personal thing, I simply don't like lawyers.

They tell lies in court which I could be jailed for.

I hope I never need a lawyer.

Friday afternoon came and went, the troops were assembled in the Squad general office by the D/I and briefed as to what we were about to do.

Very straightforward, no niceties, park the cars on Shettleston Road out of sight of the target flat and walk the short distance to the close which was the first entrance on the right in Academy Street.

It went like clockwork, the controlled entry system was still disabled, six of us climbed the stairs almost silently, as we neared the front door, the damned thing opened and a male emerged onto the landing.

No need to be asked twice, he was bundled back inside and we piled into the flat.

Instead of having to force the door with the risk of a short delay there, thus giving the suspect the opportunity of flushing the drugs away down the toilet pan, we were in.

I took hold of the man who had tried to leave whilst the rest of the team ran along a short hallway and into the living-room.

There was a lot of shouting and swearing for a few minutes, but the troops soon calmed down and secured the situation. This wasn't 'Taggart' or 'The Bill' type of rubbish. Real police officers do actually swear.

The main man was found in the living-room along with the female I'd seen previously. They were the only three people in the house besides us.

The dealer was handcuffed to the rear as he was deemed to be violent and therefore a risk to the officers.

The tall skinny male was also 'cuffed, his wrists were so thin he could probably have slipped out of them with little or no bother.

I gave them another wee squeeze just to be sure. He complained about the pain being caused to his wrists so I squeezed them again.

See Glasgow? See human rights? See me? See a real bastard.

The female was told to sit on a couch with her hands on her knees and not to move a muscle. She did exactly that. See common sense?

Our man was beginning to growl a bit as he'd obviously recognised the D/I, no love lost there.

The search was really easy and straightforward, about sixty tenner-bags of heroin were recovered from a drawer in the livingroom sideboard, a tick-list was also found there. (A list of names and nicknames with amounts of money alongside them denoting who owed how much for drugs yet to be paid for.)

Not a difficult case to prove in court.

The skinny boy had two bags in his trousers pocket and the female had nothing.

Quite interestingly the dealer and the wee female had the same surname, brother and sister? No, they were cousins and she now lived with her junkie boyfriend in nearby Old Shettleston Road which is only about five minutes walk from Academy Street.

She and her headcase of a cousin were very close friends, they'd been brought up together by his mother in Pollok even going through school together as they were about the same age.

This man was very fond of his wee cousin.

The business of the search being completed in about one hour, we did all of the necessary bumph and took our leave.

The D/I would report the case himself and we would let the judicial process take its course.

A nice easy wee turn which actually for once went off as planned.

About a month or perhaps two months later I read a report of a drugs death which had occurred in Shettleston about a week before.

It was the wee female junkie from Old Shettleston Road, a *'run of the mill'* drugs overdose in her flat. She'd been discovered lying on the kitchen floor by her skinny boyfriend with a needle sticking into her left arm.

There were no suspicious circumstances surrounding the death and it was written off. *'No further enquiry'*.

I wondered at the time if her drugs dealing cousin would feel any remorse as a pound to a penny the heroin would have been sourced from him.

It's a funny old world, two weeks later the skinny boyfriend was found by a neighbour lying dead on the kitchen floor of the flat he'd shared with his equally now deceased girlfriend.

The needle was sticking into his left arm also.

It was of course an accidental overdose of heroin.

I heard a story years later from a man in Shettleston, he said that the cousin and a couple of his cronies had called at the flat in Old Shettleston Road, held the skinny boy down and injected him with a lethally high dose of heroin.

It may be true or it may be a complete and utter lie, the fact is I simply don't know the answer to that one and never will.

Then again, the man from Academy Street was given to acts of extreme violence wasn't he?

Glossary

Ah	I
Aye	Yes
Aye mibbe	Yes maybe
Ane ae	One of
Ah'm ah	Am I
Aw	All
Alane	Alone
Burd	Girlfriend or female
'a Body'	police jargon for arrested person
Canny	astute/ shrewd
Diked	avoided work
Daen	doing
Faither	father
Flier	leave work early
Got the jail	was arrested
Grass	informant
Gonnie	going to/intend to
Hoose	house
Hud	had
Hing	thing
Hink	think
Huv ye goat	do you have
Junkie	drug addict

Glossary

Mibbe	maybe/perhaps
The Morra	tomorrow
My man's	my husband's
Nae	no/none
Ned	minor criminal
Nane	none
Plainer	plain clothed police officer
Rattling	withdrawal symptoms requiring drugs
Smack	controlled drug diamorphine (heroin)
Steamie	public wash-house
Turn	criminal act/police operation
Toffee	easy/simple
Tar-brush	dark skinned person
Tan	break into
Tanned	broken into
Tout	informant
Tenner	ten pounds sterling
Whit	what
Weegie	glaswegian
Wrang	wrong
Windae	window
Your teas oot	you've lost

Acknowledgments

Writer: William Greenshields

Editor: Laura Barbara Kincaid

Design and Production: Michael Dunbar